AUSTRALIA— TRADITIONAL MUSIC IN ITS HISTORY

AUSTRALIA —
TRADITIONAL MUSIC IN ITS HISTORY

By Ruth L. Hausman

THE CHRISTOPHER PUBLISHING HOUSE
NORTH QUINCY, MASSACHUSETTS 02171

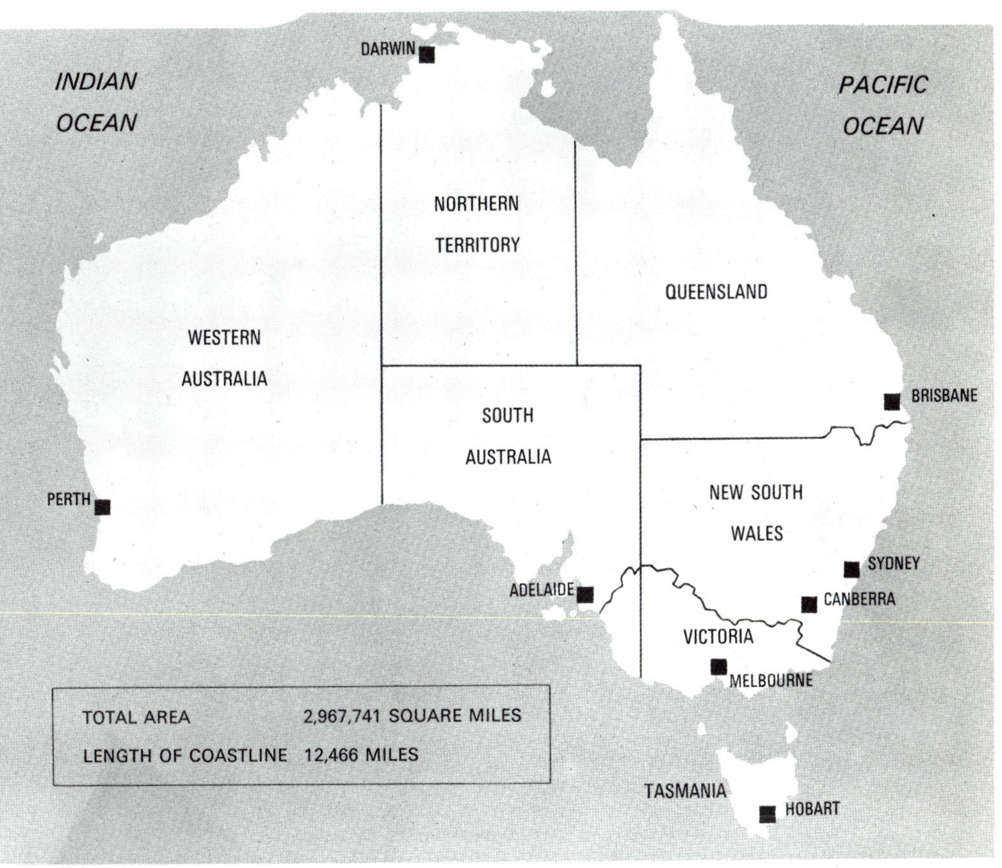

Map of Australia showing the six states and their capitals, including Tasmania (the Northern Territory is not yet a state).

INTRODUCTION

"Aussie Woman Writes United States History" was the heading that recently confronted me in a Philadelphia newspaper. Reading on, I found that a certain Australian radio and television personality was the scriptwriter for "A Nation Is Born," a sound and light production to be given nightly at Independence Hall in Philadelphia. It was here, on July 4, 1776, that the Declaration of Independence was signed and the thirteen original colonies became "free and independent states." According to my logic, if an Australian can write United States history, there is no reason why a United States citizen cannot become so interested and steeped in Australian lore as to authentically compile *Australia— Traditional Music in Its History.*

This has been an enlightening and most enjoyable experience to not only become better acquainted with, but also to develop an increasing respect for a relatively young and most interesting country, occupying an entire continent; one that geographically lies between the Pacific and Indian Oceans and is definitely in the Asian and Pacific sphere, yet in outlook and way of life adheres to the European and American cultures.

What better and more interesting way is there to narrate a nation's history than through its music! By relating the two it is possible to show life as it was lived, historic events as they happened, with music as a reflection of these happenings, whether great or small.

The Australian material divided itself readily into three main chapters. "The Pre-Colonial Era," because of the aborigines, encompassed unnumbered centuries. Rather than devote many pages at the beginning of the book to a more or less detailed recital of Stone Age living, you will find that, after a short account there, the customs and music of the aborigines are relegated to some closing pages of the book—a fitting "coda" to a history involving two races with differing cultures trying to find a common ground of understanding.

It is always difficult to decide how many or how few to include of the repetitive aboriginal chants, for they may be highly interesting to some and highly uninteresting to others. We hope that we have included enough for the former and not too many for the latter—just enough to whet their appetite. For those interested, fortunately there are periodicals and books for them to delve more deeply into the subject.

The second section, "The Colonial Era—The Nineteenth Century," covers a little more than a hundred years. Little if any originality is found in the melodies of the songs. Folk tunes and music hall ballads were transplanted from European countries, chiefly from England, Ireland and a few from Scotland, to a far distant and non-European land. Similarly, this had happened in the United States, Canada, New Zealand, South Africa and Latin America. It is the text of the songs that makes them peculiarly Australian, depicting sometimes truthfully and sometimes to an exaggerated degree the way of life in the convict camps, the huts and shearing sheds of the sheep and cattle stations, or on the roads (if they existed) and countryside in the bush. We will not quibble as to the musical or poetic worth of these traditional songs; some are superior to others. We are grateful to those who have kept alive this musical heritage as a picture of Australia in the nineteenth century.

After only two hundred years since the landing of Captain Cook on its shores, "Twentieth Century Australia" exhibits continuous growth in every direction, realizing its many possibilities nationally while achieving recognition as a major power internationally. No matter how much or how little is reported in the field of traditional music in the present century, "Waltzing Matilda" overshadows them all.

Popular music today in Australia is highly imitative of whatever is in vogue in the United States, whether jazz, swing, calypso or rock and roll. Lyrics may be adapted to fit the local scene, a habit perhaps inherited from their forebears.

If some important aspects of Australian history are only touched upon, perhaps even omitted, it is because these events were not celebrated in song. If they were, these ballads have not survived.

The accompaniments, with the exception of "Waltzing Matilda," "The Three Drovers," "Carol of the Birds" and "An Australian Christmas Carol" have been arranged by the author, bearing in mind the simple pianistic ability of some of the users of this book.

Simple chordings are suggested for chord organ, guitar and auto-harp.

With grateful acknowledgment to all who contributed in any way to making this book a reality: to

A. P. Elkin, Editor of Oceania, University of Sydney, for permission to use:

1. *Djerag—The Shark (Marauwa)* from *Arnhem Land Music Part II—A Musical Survey* by Trevor A. Jones, *Oceania,* Vol. 26, No. 4 (June, 1956), p. 318.

2. The article describing the corroboree on the final pages of this book, from *Arnhem Land Music* by A. P. Elkin in *Oceania,* Vol. 24, No. 2 (December, 1953), pp. 92-93.

T. G. H. Strehlow, Reader in Australian Linguistics, University of Adelaide, for permission to use the verses of *Honey Ant Song of Ljaba (Makerenben)* from *Songs of Central Australia* by T. G. H. Strehlow and published by Angus and Robertson, Cremorne Jct. N. S. W. Australia, 1971.

Joyce McGrath, Art and Music Librarian, State Library of Victoria, Melbourne.

R. E. Baré, Allans Music Pty. Ltd., Melbourne, for permission to use *An Australian Christmas Carol.*

John S. Manifold, compiler of *The Penguin Australian Song Book.*

Helen Blakemore, Secretary, The Australian-New Zealand Society of New York, Inc., New York.

R. R. Paton, National Library of Australia, Australian Consulate-General, New York.

Brian McKibbin, Australian News and Information Bureau, New York.

Alan Jabbour, Archive of Folk Song, Reference Department, Music Division, Library of Congress, Washington, D. C.

The many willing and efficient librarians at the

1. Free Library of Philadelphia, the Central Library and the Wynne-field Branch.

2. Libraries of the University of Pennsylvania, including the Charles Patterson VanPelt Library, the Museum Library, and the Otto E. Albrecht Music Library.

Jane W. Tyas, "gal Friday," and incidentally, my niece.

CONTENTS

ILLUSTRATIONS

Mustering cattle in Australia

*(Courtesy of "Australian Panorama" – an Australian
News and Information Bureau Publication)*

AUSTRALIA – TRADITIONAL MUSIC IN ITS HISTORY

PRE-COLONIAL AUSTRALIA

The Aborigines

Early Explorers and Navigators:
  "Haul Away, Joe"

Captain Cook Lands at Botany Bay:
  "Blow the Man Down"

A history of Australia begins properly when the aborigines, still a people without a name, came to this unknown land. The time of the migrations is presumed to have been when there were land bridges between Australia, the mainland of Asia and the intervening islands—perhaps 1000 B.C. or even earlier. Some anthropologists assert that these brown-skinned people came from as far away as the Caucasus or northern India, while others claim that their origin was Ceylon, Malaya or northern Japan.

The encroaching seas to the north of Australia eventually made it impossible for these natives to have any contact with their homeland, wherever it may have been. In Australia they evolved a Stone Age culture of their own. Theirs was a nomadic existence, with no knowledge of seed-bearing plants and no domestic animals except their dog, the dingo. These primitive people were food gatherers and hunters, ever moving on to "greener pastures" for their sustenance.

The life of the aborigine was, and still is, a tribal one. Their tribe is not a political unit but a territorial and linguistic group with its own particular customs. Having no chief, their male elders dominate the social and religious life of the tribe. It is they who, with unswerving discipline, enforce the worship of ancestors and the social activities decreed by their forbears. Being a preliterate people, it is again the older men who diligently teach the young men the chants and dances by which their gods were appeased. Always committed to memory, tribal myths and legends, usually lengthy and perhaps full of intimate details, are told round the camp fire at night or at a "secret" site on sacred ground.

Their traditional songs and dances may be either sacred or secular. All members of the tribe participate in the corroboree, which may continue night after night for several weeks. The music is highly repetitive but, to the aborigines, never monotonous. A limited number of instruments accompany the singing and dancing.

In later years, a concerted effort by research teams to record the traditional culture of these peoples has resulted in studies and musical recordings now available. A resume of these including several authentic chants, will be found in a closing chapter of this book.

For many thousands of years the aborigines were the sole inhabitants of this huge continent. No others approached by land or sea. Marco Polo, Asian and Polynesian navigators discovered certain islands of the Pacific but evidently were never interested enough to search out explicitly the great southern continent, of which men even then suspected its existence.

Before the seventeenth century, the discovery of Australia by Europeans is clouded with doubts. With highly questionable proofs, Portuguese and Spanish mariners laid claim to certain discoveries in the area. Of a certainty, Torres, a Spaniard, passed through the strait in 1606 just north of Australia, a body of water which today bears his name.

The entrance of the Dutch into the East as explorers, merchants and colonists altered the then existing incomplete and inaccurate maps of the western coast of Australia. The Dutch mariners charted this part of the continent enroute to the Dutch East Indies, meanwhile reporting it as a most inhospitable land and naming it New Holland. In 1642, Abel Tasman, dispatched by the Dutch East India Company, set out from Java to explore southward, hoping to find new markets for trade, including a more convenient route to South America. The two ships under his command finally sighted land and anchored in an unknown harbor. Going ashore, they planted a flag of the Netherlands and took possession of a land now called Tasmania. At that time they named it Van Diemen's Land to honor Anthony Van Diemen, the distinguished governor-general of the Dutch East Indies at that time.

No matter what the nationality of a sailor, he always had his work songs or shanties as he hauled away on the ropes, one of the laborious jobs at sea. The shanty repertory of these old salts increased as they learned from each other, realizing, consciously or unconsciously,

Aboriginal Dancers.
(Courtesy of Australian News and Information Bureau)

that a song is simply "another hand on the rope," no matter what the language.

"Haul Away, Joe" shows its great age by its simplicity and the use of the word "bowline" (identical with the "foresheet" of today, a term that immediately dates a shanty as sixteenth or early seventeenth century).

A "short-drag" shanty was used during hauling jobs that took perhaps only a few pulls, but they had to be extra good ones. In singing this, all hands gave a tremendous pull on the word "Joe," with an occasional grunt substituted for the last word.

HAUL AWAY, JOE

HAUL AWAY, JOE

Solo   1. Way, haul away, we'll haul away the bowline;
Chorus   Way, haul away, we'll haul away, Joe!

Solo   2. Way, haul away, the packet is a-rolling;
Chorus   Way, haul away, we'll haul away, Joe!

Solo   3. Once I had a Spanish girl; she nearly drove me crazy;
Chorus   Way, haul away, we'll haul away, Joe!

Solo   4. Now I've got an Irish girl, and she is just a daisy;
Chorus   Way, haul away, we'll haul away, Joe!

Solo   5. Way, haul away, we'll bust or break or bend her;
Chorus   Way, haul away, we'll haul away, Joe!

From 1642 until 1770, little of consequence happened relative to the exploration of New Holland. Meantime, in 1769 the orbit of the planet Venus was expected to cross the face of the sun, with the South Pacific area being the most favorable location for watching the phenomenon. The Royal Society of London requested the Admiralty to furnish a ship with trained observers and proper instruments to set sail for the Pacific. The request was granted and James Cook, an already proven leader of seamen, an expert cartographer and a capable astronomer, was selected to command the expedition.

The passage of Venus successfully observed, Cook set his course to the south, following instructions to find, if possible, the legendary New Holland, about which the Europeans were increasingly curious. From New Zealand, which he explored and charted, he resolved to sail westward "until we fall in with the east coast of New Holland, and then to follow the direction of that coast to the northward, or whatever direction it might take us, until we arrive at the northern extremity." His own words show that his plan was a logical one; later events prove it to have been a very happy one.

In several weeks they sighted land, sailed north for a short distance along the east coast of New Holland and, on April, 30, 1770, anchored in what is now called Botany Bay, so named because of the variety of plant life found there. Continuing their voyage northward for four months, they took possession, in the words of Captain Cook, "of the whole eastern coast from latitude 38 degrees to this place 10½ degrees latitude south in right of His Majesty George the Third." He renamed the area New South Wales.

If, as the historians tell us, the sailors on the Admiralty ships were not permitted to sing shanties, there must have been off-duty hours when these robust men lustily sang forecastle songs, even an occasional folk ballad from the homeland. Inadvertently interspersed among these might have been some well known work songs, perhaps even one of the most popular shanties of the late eighteenth century: "Blow the Man Down," of English origin.

*"Blow" meant "knock." In those days, sailors were sometimes knocked out and "shanghaied" onto a ship which was having difficulty getting a crew.

**Halyard: a rope or tackle for hoisting and lowering sails, flags, etc.

BLOW THE MAN DOWN

1. As I was walking down Paradise Street,
   With a Weigh Heigh! Blow the man down!
   A pretty young damsel I chanced to meet,
   Give me some time to blow the man down!

2. She was round in the counter and bluff in the bow
   With a Weigh Heigh! Blow the man down!
   So I took in all sail and cried, "Way enough now!"
   Give me some time to blow the man down!

3. So I tailed her my flipper and took her in tow.
   With a Weigh Heigh! Blow the man down!
   And yardarm to yardarm away we did go.
   Give me some time to blow the man down!

4. But as we were going, she said unto me,
   With a Weigh Heigh! Blow the man down!
   "There's a spanking full rigger just ready for sea,"
   Give me some time to blow the man down!

5. But as soon as that packet was clear of the bar,
   With a Weigh Heigh! Blow the man down!
   The mate knocked me down with the end of a spar,
   Give me some time to blow the man down!

6. So I give you fair warning before we belay,
   With a Weigh Heigh! Blow the man down!
   Don't ever take heed of what pretty girls say,
   Give me some time to blow the man down!

Australia: *Coat of arms.* Design shows kangaroo and emu supporting a shield surrounded by wattle branches.

A group of aborigines overlooking Sydney Harbour – from a drawing made in 1792.

THE COLONIAL ERA — THE NINETEENTH CENTURY

The First White Settlers — The Convicts
  "The Convict Maid" — "Van Diemen's Land"
  "Moreton Bay" — "Botany Bay"

Transportation to Australia
  "We're Bound For South Australia"

Discovery of Gold
  "Look Out Below!"
  "With My Swag All on My Shoulder"

Immigration
  "Billy Barlow in Australia"

Problems With Land
  "O Give Me a Hut" — "Eumerella Shore"

The Bushrangers
  "Bold Jack Donahue" — "The Wild Colonial Boy"
  "Ballad of Ben Hall's Gang" — "Death of Ned Kelly"

Workers in the Bush at the Sheep and Cattle Stations
  "Click Go the Shears" — "Widgegoara Joe"
  "The Sheepwasher" — "The Ram of Dalby"
  "The Banks of the Condamine" — "The Old Bark Hut"
  "The Dying Stockman"

The Bullockies
  "Bullocky O" — "Bill, the Bullocky"

The Drovers
  "The Queensland Drover" — "The Drover's Dream"
  "Ladies of Brisbane"

New South Wales was too far distant for the English to be interested in going there to establish colonies, but at that time their jails were greatly overcrowded and New South Wales seemed to be an expedient place to which to send their convicts. They were not consciously planting a colony so much as ridding themselves of a problem. Previously they had transported their undesirables to North America, but since the American Revolution these doors were closed to them.

Accordingly, in 1787, eleven vessels set sail from Portsmouth, England, with some 750 convicts aboard, the majority being male with about 200 females. On arriving in New South Wales in 1788, Governor Arthur Phillip, in charge of the experiment, moved the location from Botany Bay to a more favorable location a short distance to the north, describing it as "the finest harbour in the world." On January 26, with appropriate but simple ceremonies, it was named in honor of Lord Sydney, Secretary of State for the Home Department, the administrative body in London responsible for the new settlement.

To clear the land for agriculture, to chop down trees for the erection of wooden huts and to unload stores of supplies from the ships were chores which any settlers have. Many problems peculiar to this colony arose, because of the character of the convicted colonists and also because of the inadequacy and irregularity of supplies coming from a far distant homeland, while the settlement was still unable to supply its own needs.

As more and more convicts arrived, Governor Phillip protested: "The sending out of the disordered and helpless clears the jails and may ease the parishes from which they are sent, but it is obvious this settlement, instead of a colony which is to support itself, will remain for years a burthen to the mother country." He pleaded with his government to send, in addition to the criminals, some honest, intelligent settlers. "We shall want some good characters to whom these people might look up."

After many and varied vicissitudes, some overcome but others still unsolved, Governor Phillip resigned in 1792 just as he saw his colony approaching a state of independence in the production of the necessities of life.

The convicts, accidentally the first white settlers in Australia, were an unruly, often rebellious group, including some notorious ruffians. They ranged from callous villains to the unfortunate weaklings of society. Apologists would state that conditions were such among the poorer classes in eighteenth and nineteenth century Great Britain that it was relatively easy to become a criminal; that the prisons were so overcrowded and living conditions so unspeakably bad that prisoners readily became hardened and sometimes deranged. These delinquents transported to Australia were London pickpockets, poachers from the English Midlands, burners of hay ricks in Ireland, all seemingly minor offenders; but also including, as their companions, many accused of the most serious crimes against society.

Their many songs relate a petty crime for which they were convicted, when this perhaps could have been only one incident in a lifetime of crime.

The women were in the minority but are represented in the "convict" folklore. The simple tune of "The Convict Maid" is similar to that of an Irish street ballad, "My Boy Willie." Willie was a sailor whose ever faithful girl has been searching for him, only to be told:

> "O, then your boy Willie, I am sorry to say,
> Has just been drowned the other day.
> On yon green island that we pass by,
> 'Twas there we laid your poor sailor boy."

Though miles apart geographically, the two songs have several things in common: their melody and a sad ending.

The Convict Maid

THE CONVICT MAID

1. You lads and lasses all attend to me
   While I relate my tale of misery;
   By hopeless love was I once betrayed,
   And now I am, alas, a Convict Maid.

2. To please my lover did I try so sore,
   That I spent upon him all my master's store,
   Who in his wrath did so loud upbraid,
   And brought before the judge this Convict Maid.

3. The judge his sentence then to me addressed,
   Which filled with agony my aching breast:
   "To Botany Bay you must be conveyed
   For seven long years to be a Convict Maid."

4. For seven long years I toil in pain and grief,
   And curse the day that I became a thief.
   Oh, had I stuck by some honest trade,
   I ne'er had been, alas, a Convict Maid.

England was particularly pleased to rid its jails of the most refractory inmates by reassigning them to its most distant penal colony, Van Diemen's Land (now Tasmania). The moral level of the prisoners transported there was very low and the disciplinary measures taken against them most severe. The stories of always hungry dogs and sharks guarding escape are numerous and most shocking.

In Tasmania today are to be seen the relics of late eighteenth and early nineteenth century prison confinement and punishment for the most unruly: leg irons, fetters and black cells for solitary confinement.

The poet of the song, "Van Diemen's Land," received rather humane treatment in comparison with the stories of some of the prisoners confined there.

Van Diemen's Land

VAN DIEMEN'S LAND

1. Come all you gallant poaching boys that ramble free of care,
   That rove out on a moonlit night with gun and dog and snare;
   The hare and lofty pheasant you have at your command,
   Never thinking of your last career upon Van Diemen's Land.

2. Poor Tommy Brown from Nottingham,
      Jack Murphy and poor Joe,
   We are three daring poachers as the gentry well does know;
   One night we were trepanned by the keepers hid in sand,
   Who for fourteen years transported us unto Van Diemen's Land.

3. The first day that they landed us upon that fatal shore,
   The free men came around us all, full twenty score or more,
   They ranked us up like horses and sold us out of hand,
   They yoked us to the ploughs
      like beasts to plough Van Diemen's Land.

4. The huts we're forced to shelter in are built of mud and clay,
   We have stinking straw for bedding, and no one can say nay;
   With fire they fence us nightly, we slumber when we can,
   But it keeps the wolves and tigers at bay upon Van Diemen's Land.

5. A girl I knew in young days, Susie Summers was her name,
   Was sent out here for fourteen years, an old hand at the game;
   Our master bought her freedom and wed her out of hand,
   And she gives us all good treatment upon Van Diemen's Land.

6. But it's often when I slumber I see the form again,
   Of a girl I knew who loved me before this time of shame;
   We walk by quiet waters, my life at her command,
   And I wake up broken hearted upon Van Diemen's Land.

7. So all you lively poaching lads, this warning take from me:
   I'd have you quit night walking and avoid bad company,
   And throw aside your guns and snares, for let me tell you plain,
   If you knew of our misfortunes, you would never poach again.

Moreton Bay was a remote penal colony north of Sydney, settled later than most in New South Wales as a placement for twice-convicted and incorrigible offenders. It had no contacts with the outside world except when a government ship arrived every second month.

Remoteness not only segregated the most unmanageable of the convicts, but also permitted the commandant and guards to perpetrate horrible atrocities as punishment. Perhaps the isolation of the settlement was enough to deprave keepers as well as those committed.

Graphically described infamies in the text of "Moreton Bay" are set to the beautiful melody of a traditional Irish ballard, "Youghal Harbour." Captain Logan, mentioned in the song, was speared in 1830, his murder attributed by some to the aborigines, but others believe the convicts were the responsible ones.

In 1830, there were approximately one thousand convicts and one hundred soldiers at the settlement. Finally there was talk of discontinuing the establishment and, in 1837, numbers were reduced to three hundred, mostly women who were employed in agriculture. The district was opened to settlers several years later, with the squatters moving in as the convicts moved out.

Moreton Bay

With much expression
ONE SUN-DAY MORN-ING, AS I WENT WALK-ING BY BRIS-BANE WAT-ERS I CHANCED TO STRAY, I
HEARD A PRIS'-NER HIS FATE BE-WAIL-ING, AS ON THE SUN-NY RIV-ER BANK HE LAY. "I
AM A NA-TIVE OF ER-IN'S IS-LAND AND BAN-ISHED NOW FROM MY NA-TIVE SHORE; THEY
TORE ME FROM MY A-GED PA-RENTS AND FROM THE MAID-EN WHOM I DO A-DORE."

MORETON BAY

1. One Sunday morning, as I went walking, by Brisbane waters
       I chanced to stray;
   I heard a pris'ner his fate bewailing, as on the sunny river bank
       he lay.
   "I am a native of Erin's island and banished now
       from my native shore;
   They tore me from my aged parents and from the maiden
       I do adore.

2. I've been a pris'ner at Port Macquarie, at Norfolk Island
       and Emu Plains,
   At Castle Hill and at cursed Toongabbie, at all those settlements
       I've worked in chains;
   But of all the places of condemnation and penal stations
       of New South Wales.
   To Moreton Bay I have found no equal;
       Excessive tyranny each day prevails.

3. For three long years I was beastly treated, and heavy irons
       on my leg I wore.
   My back with flogging is lacerated and often painted
       with my crimson gore.
   And many a man from downright starvation lies mouldering now
       underneath the clay;
   And Captain Logan he had us mangled
       at the triangles of Moreton Bay.

4. Like the Egyptians and ancient Hebrews
       we were oppressed under Logan's yoke,
   Till a native man, lying there in ambush, did give our tyrant
       his mortal stroke.
   My fellow prisoners, be exhilarated that all such monsters
       such a death may find!
   And when from bondage we are liberated our former sufferings
       shall fade from mind!"

Although short lived as a settlement, "Botany Bay" as a name survived for many years as a synonym for the whole penal settlement.

The origin of the song titled "Botany Bay" is controversial, as some authorities insist that it is not a bona fide convict song but a parody of the "real thing." It was popularized by the music hall singer, David Belasco James, in the music comedy, "Little Jack Shepherd" (London 1885; Melbourne 1886).

Botany Bay

BOTANY BAY

1. Farewell to old England forever,
   Farewell to my old pals as well;
   Farewell to the well known old Bailee,
   Where 1 used for to cut such a swell.

Chorus
   Singing too-ral-li oo-ral-li ad-dity
   Singing too-ral-li oo-ral li-ay;
   Singing too-ral-li oo-ral-li ad-dity,
   Singing too-ral-li oo-ral-li-ay.

2. There's the Captain as is our Commander,
   There's the bo'sun and all the ship's crew,
   There's the first and second class passengers,
   Knows what we poor convicts go through.

Chorus

3. 'Taint leavin' old England we cares about,
   'Taint cos we mispels what we knows,
   But becos all we light-fingered gentry
   Hops around with a log on our toes.

Chorus

4. For seven long years I'll be staying here,
   For seven long years and a day,
   For meeting a cove in an area
   And taking his ticker away.

Chorus

5. Oh, had I the wings of a turtle-dove!
   I'd soar on my pinions so high,
   Slap bang to the arms of my Polly love
   And in her sweet presence I'd die.

Chorus

6. Now, all my young Dookies and Duchesses,
   Take warning from what I've to say,
   Mind all is your own as you touchesses,
   or you'll find us in Botany Bay.

Chorus

Governors came and departed, bringing order and sometimes disorder to the settlement. The New South Wales Corps, a military group organized in England, was assigned to Sydney. Many of the officers in the group were permitted to acquire land and to have the convicts as free laborers.

Except in the case of certain political prisoners, emancipation was one of the rewards to the criminals for good behavior while performing useful services. Grants of land were sometimes awarded to these free men.

The whole structure in New South Wales was already but slowly changing. In addition to the penal colony there were the government personnel, including the military. The number of free settlers was steadily if not spectacularly increasing, some receiving grants of land while others were merely squatters, demanding their rights. Children of the convicts were also among the free citizenry.

By the early nineteenth century the settlement had grown but was still confined to the area in and around Sydney. Eventually, after several lesser attempts, the circumnavigation and charting of the entire coastline of the huge continent was accomplished in 1803 by Michael Flinders. Proving it to be one vast island, it was no longer appropriate to term the western area New Holland and the eastern sector New South Wales. One name was agreed upon for the entire continent and, in 1817, the name AUSTRALIA (from the Latin "Australis," meaning "Southern") was officially adopted. It was the same Michael Flinders who was responsible for the suggestion of the new name.

In 1813, a way was found over the Blue Mountains west of Sydney. Exploration to the western plains, to the outback, and to the far flung reaches of the continent had begun.

The settlement continued to expand and prosper. New South Wales was the original colony. Van Diemen's Land (Tasmania) was given similar status in 1825, followed in 1829 by a colony on the Swan River, which later became Western Australia. South Australia was recognized as a separate colony in 1834, while Victoria, formerly known as Port Phillip District, became independent of New South Wales soon after. In 1859, Queensland became the sixth and youngest colony.

Aspirations toward a free society were quite pronounced in this developing continent. The convict group gradually decreased in New South Wales and Tasmania. The transfer of prisoners to the former ceased in 1840, to the latter in 1852. Happily, all that remains today of the penal system are a few ruins.

Australia, its survival and progress, was dependent on ships, the only transportation then available to and from this far distant continent. The journey was long and hazardous. Wind and weather contributed to a good or bad passage; the sea worthiness of the vessel was a most important factor for safe arrival. The first convict ships took approximately nine months for the trip; the sailing vessels in the 1850's averaged about 80 days.

Ships carrying cargo and passengers, sailing around the Horn or the Cape of Good Hope, or perhaps traveling from points north in the Pacific, made Sydney one of their ports of call. Whether in Sydney, London or San Francisco, to mention just a few of the busy waterfronts of the world, sailors might be heard singing lustily, with strong rhythm, as they hoisted the anchor: "We're Bound For South Australia."

We're Bound For South Australia

WE'RE BOUND FOR SOUTH AUSTRALIA

1. Solo   Oh, South Australia's my native home.
   Chorus Heave away! Heave away!
   Solo   Oh, South Australia's my native home.
   Chorus We're bound for South Australia.
           Heave away! Heave away!
           Oh, heave away, you ruler king,
           We're bound for South Australia.

2. Solo   There ain't but one thing grieves my mind.
   Chorus Heave away! Heave away!
   Solo   To leave my dear wife and child behind.
   Chorus We're bound for South Australia., etc.

Solo lines only

3.   I see my wife standing on the quay.
          The tears do start as she waves to me.

4.   I'll tell you the truth and I tell you no lie;
          If I don't love that girl I hope I may die.

The discovery of gold in 1851 was a major and most momentous event in the history of Australia. Almost overnight, from New South Wales and other sections of the continent, the population was on the move into Victoria. Labor deserted the sheep and cattle stations; shopkeepers, sailors and professional men abandoned their tasks for the lure of gold.

Adventurers soon began arriving from all parts of the world. California forty-niners, Texans and New Englanders were some of the representatives from the United States; the English, Irish, Italians and Hungarians were just a sampling of the Europeans. In a short time, the population of Victoria had more than tripled. The small hamlet of Melbourne for a while was the largest city in Australia. To this town's British traditions were soon added strong American influences in both its social and industrial life. As the gold fever declined, the ex-gold diggers finally merged with the community as barbers, laborers, bartenders, merchants and drivers of coaches.

The political and social consequences of the gold rush were equally as important as the wealth acquired by the young colonies. Many of the European immigrants who arrived at that time had been malcontents in their home countries and had been involved in revolutionary upheavals there. Augmenting those Australians already dissenting with existing conditions, they had a strong influence in bringing about much needed governmental reforms in the colonies. New South Wales, Victoria, Southern Australia and Tasmania had attained responsible self government by 1856, including the establishment of elected legislative assemblies. Similar agreements were later formulated for Western Australia and Queensland.

The miners were not the only ones attracted to the goldfields. Professional entertainers, among them Thatcher, Mulholland, Chanson and Coxon (just to name a few), found the miners to be a most appreciative audience in more ways than one. They popularized, at that time, appropriate words usually of their own creation, set to melodies of current hit tunes from overseas.

"Look Out Below" has a text by Charles Thatcher; the melody is that of "The Pirate King."

LOOK OUT BELOW!

1. A young man left his native town,
   Through trade being slack at home.
   To seek his fortune in this land
   He crossed the briny foam.

2. And when he came to the Lachlan,
   His heart was in a glow,
   To hear the sound of the windlasses,
   And the cry: "Look out below!"

3. Where'er he turned his wondering eyes,
   Strange sights he did behold
   Of full and plenty in the land
   And the magic power of gold.

4. He says: "Now I am young and strong,
   And a-digging I will go,
   For I like the sound of the windlasses,
   And the cry: "Look out below!"

5. So now he's settled down again
   With a charming little wife.
   He says: "There's nothing can come up
   To a jolly digger's life."

6. Ask him if he'll go home again
   And he'll quickly answer: "No,"
   For he likes the sound of the windlasses
   And the cry: "Look out below!"

"With My Swag All on My Shoulder," set to an old Irish tune, has an interesting text *about* an immigrant, but possibly not *by* an immigrant.

With My Swag All On My Shoulder

WITH MY SWAG ALL ON MY SHOULDER

1. When first I left old Ireland's shore,
   the yarns that we were told
Of how the folks in far Australia
   could pick up lumps of gold!
How gold dust lay in all the streets
   and miner's right was free!
"Hurrah!" I told my loving friends,
   "That's just the place for me!"

Chorus
   With my swag all on my shoulder, black billy in my hand,
   I'll travel the bushes of Australia like a trueborn Irishman.

2. When first we reached Port Melbourne,
    we were all prepared to slip
And bar the captain and the mate;
    all hands abandoned ship.
And all the girls of Melbourne town threw up
    their arms with joy,
Hurrooing and exclaiming, "Here comes my Irish boy!"

Chorus
    With his swag all on his shoulder, black billy in his hand,
    He'll travel the bushes of Australia like a trueborn Irishman.

3. We made our way into Geelong,
    then north to Ballarat,
Where some of us grew mighty thin,
    and some grew sleek and fat.
Some tried their luck at Bendigo
    and some at Fiery Creek;
I made my fortune in a day
    and blued it in a week.

Chorus
    With my swag all on my shoulder, black billy in my hand,
    I travelled the bushes of Australia like a trueborn Irishman.

4. For many years I wandered round
    to each new field about,
And made and spent full many a pound
    'til alluvial petered out.
And then for any job of work
    I was prepared to try,
But now I've found the tucker track;
    I'll stay there 'til I die.

Chorus
    With my swag all on my shoulder, black billy in my hand,
    I'll travel the bushes of Australia like a trueborn Irishman.

Immigration is, and has been through the years, of paramount importance to the development of Australia. The aborigines were accidentally the first migrants, followed many centuries later by those unwilling colonists, the convicts. Free settlers in the early nineteenth century emigrated from Britain in such small numbers that in 1822 a slogan, "Populate or Perish" was adopted. When it was demonstrated that there was money to be made in wool, some men of property in Scotland and England left their homeland to settle in Australia. The gold rush of the 1850's brought all types of humanity from many European and American countries. When times were good, when there was more work than workers and jobs were easy to get, mass migration was promulgated. Varying inducements, including a "bounty" system, brought these "New Australians" to work and live alongside of the "Old Australians."

However, in the latter half of the nineteenth century, after the gold fever had subsided, jobs were at a premium and the influx of immigrants subsided. In addition to some ne'er-do-wells who filtered into the country, there was a steady flow from the United Kingdom of new and sometimes affluent colonists, coming for their own personal reasons and at their own expense.

"Billy Barlow in Australia" recites some of the trials and tribulations of one of the less fortunate immigrants.

Billy Barlow In Australia

BILLY BARLOW IN AUSTRALIA

1. When I was at home I was down on my luck,
   And I earned a poor living by driving a truck.
   But old aunt died and left me a thousand—"Oho!
   I'll start on my travels," said Billy Barlow.
   Chorus
   Oh, dear, lackaday oh,
   So off to Australia came Billy Barlow.

2. When to Sydney I got, there a merchant I met,
   Who said he would teach me a fortune to get.
   He had cattle and sheep past the colony's bounds,
   Which he sold with the station for my thousand pounds.
   Chorus
   Oh, dear, lackaday oh,
   He gammoned the cash out of Billy Barlow.

3. So I got my supplies and I gave him my bill,
   And for my station started, my pockets to fill;
   But by bushrangers met, with my traps they made free,
   Took my horse and left Billy tied up to a tree.
   Chorus
   Oh, dear, lackaday oh,
   "I shall die of starvation," thought Billy Barlow.

4. At last I got loose, and I then did repair
   For my station once more, and at length I got there.
   But a few days before that, some thieves, you must know,
   Had speared all the cattle of Billy Barlow.
   Chorus
   Oh, dear, lackaday oh,
   "It's a beautiful country," says Billy Barlow.

5. And for nine months before, no rain there had been,
   So never a blade of grass was to be seen.
   One third of my wethers the scab they had got,
   And the other two thirds had just died of the rot.
   Chorus
   Oh, dear, lackaday oh,
   "I shall soon be a settler," said Billy Barlow.

6. I'm in Sydney, insolvent, in poverty's toil.
   I've no cattle for salting, no sheep for to boil.
   I can't get a job, though to any I'd stoop,
   If 'twas only the making of portable soup.
   Chorus
   Oh, dear, lackaday oh,
   Pray give some employment to Billy Barlow.

If Australia had an overabundance of anything, it was land. Not foreseeing the future, it was easy and expedient in the early days to make grants of land to some freed convicts, to some in the military, and to those willing to leave their homeland to settle in a far distant and unfamiliar continent, while squatters settled on land without acquiring title to it. Soon the best lands were in the hands of a few, some of whom acquired large estates. The squatters many times were among the privileged group.

When the government found this lack of planning most inconvenient as the population increased, fair and unfair laws were passed to rectify a bad situation. Oliver Cromwell's words describing the laws of England are most appropriate to describe the passage of land legislation in Australia: "an ungodly jumble."

In 1861, John Robertson proposed two bills to bring order out of chaos. Passed by Parliament, the Acts were greeted with rousing approbation by the squatters and would-be farmers or free selectors alike. However, it was soon found that there were many inequities to be resolved by both parties, with the squatters again in the better position.

The lyricist of "O Give Me a Hut" must have written the words in the first burst of enthusiasm, only to be disillusioned later.

O Give Me A Hut

O GIVE ME A HUT

1. Ye sons of industry, to you I belong,
   And to you I would dedicate a verse or a song,
   To rejoice at the vic'try John Robertson's won,
   Now the Land Bill is passed and good times have come.

   Chorus
   Then give me a hut in my own native land,
   Or a tent in Australia where the tall gum trees stand;
   No matter how far in the bush it may be,
   If a girl like Kate Kelly would share it with me.

2. No more with our swags through the bush need we roam,
   Imploring of charity to give us a home,
   For the land is unfettered, and we may reside
   In a home of our own by some clear waterside.

   Chorus

3. We will plant our own garden and sow our own field,
   And eat of the fruits which industry will yield,
   And be independent, as long as we have strived,
   Tho' those who have ruled us the right long denied.

   Chorus

"Eumerella Shore" first appeared as a poem in the *Launceston Examiner,* a local Australian publication. This text could be either an authentic creation by a free selector (would-be-farmer), or might possibly be a humorous slander perpetrated by a squatter, always the enemy of the free selector. The latter was known generally as a respected and law abiding citizen.

The tune is definitely related to "Darling Nelly Gray" and "The Little Old Log Cabin in the Lane," which was parodied by the American cowboy as "The Little Old Log Shanty on the Plain."

Eumerella Shore

MORE, FOR YOU'RE RUN-NING, RUN-NING, RUN-NING ON THE DUFF-ER'S PIECE OF
LAND, FREE SE-LEC-TED ON THE EU-ME-REL-LA SHORE.

EUMERELLA SHORE

1. There's a long green gully on the Eumerella Shore.
   Where I've lounged through many is the day.
   All by my selection I have acres by the score,
   So I'll unyoke my bullocks from the dray.
   To my cattle I do say, you may feed, feed away,
   But you'll never be impounded any more,
   For you're running, running, running on the duffer's piece of land,
   Free selected on the Eumerella Shore.

2. When the moon is shining bright and has climbed
       the mountain high,
   We will saddle up our horses and away.
   We will steal the squatter's cattle by the darkness of the night,
   And we'll brand at the dawn of the day.
   And now my pretty calf at the squatter you may laugh,
   But you'll never see your owner any more.
   For you're running, running, running on the duffer's piece of land,
   Free selected on the Eumerella Shore.

3. And when we get the swag, we'll steal the squatter's nag,
   And we'll sell him at some distant, inland town.
   And when we get the cash, oh, we chaps will cut a dash
   For the doing of the squatter so brown.
   To John Robertson we say, you've been leading us astray,
   And we never can believe you any more;
   For we chaps can get a livin' far easier by thieven'
   Than by farming on the Eumerella Shore.

The first bushrangers (bush bandits) were convicts who escaped to the outback, raiding the lonely farm settlers and robbing any travelers they might find on the road.

One of the earliest of the bushrangers to be celebrated in song was "Bold Jack Donahue," who was transported from Ireland for "intent to commit a felony," and who is made to appear most virtuous in spite of his law breaking activities.

Bold Jack Donahue

BOLD JACK DONAHUE

1. There was a valiant highwayman of courage and renown,
   Who scorned to live in slavery or humble to the Crown;
   In Dublin city fair and free where first his breath he drew,
   'Twas there they christened him the brave and bold Jack Donahue.

2. He scarce had been transported unto the Australian shore,
   When he took to the highway as he had done before;
   And every week in the newspapers was published something new,
   Concerning all the valiant deeds of bold Jack Donahue.

3. As Donahue was cruising one summer afternoon,
   Little was his notion that his death would be so soon,
   When to his surprise the horse-police appeared in his view,
   And in quick time they did advance upon Jack Donahue.

4. The sergeant of the horse-police discharged his carbine,
   And called aloud on Donahue to fight or to resign;
   "I'd rather range these hills around like wolf or kangaroo,
   Than work one hour for the government,"
       cried bold Jack Donahue.

5. Six rounds he fought the horse-police until that fatal ball,
   Which pierced his heart with cruel smart caused Donahue to fall.
   The sergeant and the corporal and all their cowardly crew,
   It took them all their time to fall the bold Jack Donahue.

6. There were Freincy, Grant, bold Robin Hood
       and Brennan and O'Hare,
   With Donahue, the bushranger, none of them could compare.
   And now he's gone to Heaven, I hope, with the saints
       and angels too.
   May the Lord have mercy on the soul of bold Jack Donahue.

Later in the century the young colonials: Jack Doolan ("The Wild Colonial Boy"), Ben Hall and Ned Kelly, with their gangs, began to outvie their predecessors. Defying the law as marauders and murderers, their names were added to the listing of folk heroes of Australia. Their admirers endowed them with virtues—courage, loyalty to a cause and defiance of the establishment—which more than offset their vices.

The most popular of the bushranger ballards was "The Wild Colonial Boy," to be found in many collections with tunes numbering over a dozen and innumerable, varying texts. Some authorities place its origin early in the nineteenth century; the text used here mentions 1861 in the days of Judge Macoboy.

The spirited chorus is common to several versions, and was sung for many years as an expression of independence when labor troubles were to the fore.

A bullock wagon carting timber in the Australian bush.

A boom-time ball at the goldfields.

The Wild Colonial Boy

Chorus
COME, ALL MY HEART-IES! WE'LL RANGE THE MOUN-TAIN-SIDE. TO-
-GETH-ER WE WILL PLUN-DER, TO-GETH-ER WE WILL RIDE. WE'LL
SCOUR A-LONG THE VAL-LEYS AND GAL-LOP O'ER THE PLAINS. WE
SCORN TO LIVE IN SLAV-ER—Y, BOUND DOWN BY I-RON CHAINS.

THE WILD COLONIAL BOY

1. There was a wild colonial youth, Jack Doolan was his name.
   Of poor but honest parents he was born in Castlemaine.
   He was his father's only hope, his mother's only joy;
   The pride of both his parents was the wild colonial boy.

Chorus
   Come, all my hearties! We'll range the mountainside.
   Together we will plunder, together we will ride.
   We'll scour along the valleys and gallop o'er the plains.
   We scorn to live in slavery bowed down with iron chains.

2. He was barely sixteen years of age when he left his father's home,
   And through Australia's sunny clime as a bushranger did roam.
   He robbed those wealthy squatters, their stocks
      he did destroy,
   A terror to the rich men was the wild colonial boy.

Chorus

3. In sixty-one this daring youth commenced his wild career.
   With a heart that knew no danger, no foeman did he fear.
   He held the Beechworth mail coach up, and robbed
      Judge Macoboy,
   Who trembled and gave up his gold to the wild colonial boy.

Chorus

4. He bade the Judge "Good morning," and told him to beware
   For he'd never rob a decent judge that acted on the square,
   But not to rob a mother of her son and only joy,
   Or you'll breed a race of outlaws like the wild colonial boy.

Chorus

5. One day as he was riding the mountainside along,
   A-listening to the little birds their pleasant laughing song,
   Three mounted troopers came in sight—Kelly, Davis and Fitzroy,
   And thought that they would capture him, the wild colonial boy.

Chorus

6. "Surrender, now, Jack Doolan! You see we're three to one.
   Surrender now, Jack Doolan, you daring highwayman!"
   But he drew a pistol from his belt and spun it like a toy.
   "I'll fight but I'll not surrender," said the wild colonial boy.

Chorus

7. He fired at Trooper Kelly and brought him to the ground,
   And in return from Davis received a mortal wound.
   All shattered through the jaws he lay still firing at Fitzroy,
   And that's the way they captured the wild colonial boy.

Chorus

Ben Hall's saga is similar and yet slightly different from that of his colleagues. He, unlike the others, had been a squatter whose lands and cattle had been confiscated by the state. In revenge, he was led to the life which brought him fame.

The melody of the song is related to the Irish "The Airy Bachelor" and "The Black Horse."

Ballad Of Ben Hall's Gang

BALLAD OF BEN HALL'S GANG

1. Come all you sons of liberty and listen to my tale;
   A story of bushranging days I will to you unveil.
   'Tis of those valiant heroes, God Bless them one and all!
   Let us sit and sing: "God save the King, Dunn, Gilbert
   　　and Ben Hall."

2. Ben Hall he was a squatter, and he owned six hundred head;
   A peaceful, quiet man was he until he met Sir Fred.
   The troopers burnt his homestead down, his cattle perished all.
   "I've all my sentence yet to earn," was the word of
   　　brave Ben Hall.

3. John Gilbert was a flash cove, and young O'Meally too,
   With Ben and Bourke and Dunn and Vane, they all were comrades
   　　true.
   They bailed the Carcoar mailcoach up and made the troopers
   　　crawl;
   There's a thousand pounds set on the heads of Dunn, Gilbert and
   　　Ben Hall.

4. From Bathurst down to Goulburn town they made the coaches
   　　stand,
   While far behind, Sir Frederick's men went labouring thro' the
   　　land.
   Then at Canowindra's best hotel they gave a public ball.
   "We don't hurt them that don't hurt us," says Dunn, Gilbert
   　　and Ben Hall.

5. They held the gold commissioner to ransom on the spot,
   But young John Vane surrendered after Mickey Bourke was shot.
   O'Meally at Goimbla did like a hero fall,
   But "We'll take the country over yet," says Dunn, Gilbert and
   　　Ben Hall.

6. They never robbed a needy man, the records go to show,
   But staunch and loyal to their mates, unflinching to the foe.
   So we'll drink a toast tonight, my lads, their memories to recall.
   Let us sit and sing: "God save the King, Dunn, Gilbert
      and Ben Hall."

The last of the bushrangers to be memorialized in song is Ned
Kelly, whose deeds were the inspiration for innumerable ballads.
   "The Death of Ned Kelly" is summarized in six stanzas by Australian John S. Manifold and set by him to an interesting traditional
melody, thus creating a simple yet worthy contribution to the folk
music of Australia.

THE DEATH OF NED KELLY

Copyright 1946 by the John Day Company. Reprinted from SELECTED VERSE by
John Manifold by permission of the John Day Company, Inc., publisher.

THE DEATH OF NED KELLY

1. Ned Kelly fought the rich men in country and in town,
   Ned Kelly fought the troopers until they ran him down.
   He thought that he had fooled them, for he was hard to find,
   But he rode into Glenrowan with the troopers close behind.

2. "Come out of that, Ned Kelly," the head zarucker calls,
   "Come out and leave your shelter, or we'll shoot it full of holes."
   "If you'd take me," says Kelly, "that's not the speech to use.
   I've lived to spite your order; I'll die the way I choose."

3. "Come out of that, Ned Kelly; you done a lawless thing.
   You robbed and fought the squatters, Ned Kelly;
       you must swing."
   "If those who rob," says Kelly, "are all condemned to die,
   You had better hang the squatters, for they've stolen
       more than I."

4. "You'd best come out, Ned Kelly, you done the Government
       wrong,
   For you hold up the coaches that bring the gold along."
   "Go tell your boss," says Kelly, "who lets the rich go free,
   That your bloody rich man's government will never govern me."

5. They burned the roof above him, they fired the walls about,
   And head to foot in armour Ned Kelly stumbled out.
   Although his guns were empty, he made them turn and flee,
   But one came in behind him and shot him in the knee.

6. And so they took Ned Kelly and hanged him in the jail,
   For he fought single-handed although in iron mail.
   And no man single-handed can hope to break the bars,
   It's a thousand like Ned Kelly who'll hoist the flag of stars.

Was the real Australia of the nineteenth century in the rapidly
expanding cities; was it in the fertile pastures of the southeastern
colonies; or was it in the lonely cattle stations of the outback or the
most remote lands back-of-the-beyond?

The Glenrowan Hotel during the siege of the Kelly gang.

It is those who settled outside the cities who are celebrated in Australian folklore, be it in prose, poetry or song. The semi-nomadic life of the bush workers spread folk songs and tales (in addition to news of the countryside) over great distances in a short time. Men were constantly on the move, driving bullock drays, shearing sheep, and "humping their swag" from job to job.

From the earliest days in the colonies, the raising of sheep and the improvement of the breed was one of the most popular and profitable industries in Australia. The sheep station was usually a sizable estate, with the owner or squatter able to become an affluent member of society, if he was not already one. The squatters were quite a mixed lot. Some had little or no capital but were endowed with a strong pioneering spirit; some were wealthy men or high officials in Sydney, using sons or overseers to run the stations in the bush if they were otherwise occupied; some were of the landed gentry from Great Britain who were attracted by the flourishing wool industry in Australia to become settlers there.

The sheep station, aside from seasonal employment for shearing and washing, was conducted with a small work force. Grass grew free for the sheep to eat; the sheep grew wool without too much trouble to anyone; the wool was sheared with no harm to the animal, who continued to grow their remunerative product; the same sheep produced offspring to continue the cycle ad infinitum. Naturally there were setbacks: years of financial depression and drought, or perhaps loss of sheep by disease or killing by dingos, the native dogs. But by and large, sheep raising was financially rewarding while providing an important staple for an expanding market.

The shearer, moving from shearing shed to shearing shed, exemplifies the days when a man could "hump his swag" or "hump his drum," carry all his possessions in a roll on his back and tramp the outback. The grazier's (squatter's) treatment of these seasonal itinerants is told graphically and sometimes truthfully in many traditional songs. Happily, the formation of labor unions later improved these conditions.

The theme of the sheepshearer is well represented in Australian folklore with "Clip Go the Shears," the best known of these songs. Along with the sketchy picture of the shearing shed runs the story of the "ringer" (a champion shearer) being displaced by a "snagger" (an inferior shearer), who luckily drew from the pen a "bare-bellied Joe" (a ewe), thus shortening his shearing time.

This is a parody of "Ring the Bell, Watchman," by the American composer, Henry Clay Work, better known for his "Grandfather's Clock."

CLICK GO THE SHEARS

CHORUS
C   F Dmin. C   G   C
MAKE THE RING-ER GO!" CLICK, GO THE SHEARS, BOY, CLICK, CLICK, CLICK!
F   C   G   C
WIDE IS THE BLOW AND HIS HANDS MOVE QUICK. THE RING-ER LOOKS A-ROUND AND IS
F   D7   G7   C F Dmin. C
BEAT-EN BY A BLOW, AND CURS-ES THE OLD SNAG-GER WITH THE BARE BEL-LIED JOE.

CLICK GO THE SHEARS

1. Out on the board, my lads, the old shearer stands,
   Grasping his shears in his thin, bony hands.
   Fixed is his gaze on a bare-bellied Joe.
   Saying, "If I get you, Joe, I'll make the ringer go!"

   Chorus
   Click go the shears, boy, click, click, click.
   Wide is the blow and his hands move quick.
   The ringer looks around and is beaten by a blow,
   And curses the old snagger with the bare-bellied Joe.

2. Out on the floor in a cane-bottomed chair,
   The boss of the board with his eyes ev'rywhere,
   Notes well each fleece as it comes to the screen,
   Paying strict attention if it's taken off clean.

   Chorus

3. There is the tar boy, awaiting on demand,
   With his tarry pot and a stick in his hand.
   Sees an old merino with a cut on his back.
   Hustles as he hears the call for: "Oh, tar here, Jack!"

   Chorus

4. Take off the belly wool and finish round the rear.
   Then go up the neck; the sheep have no fear.
   Clean round the horns and the first shoulder down;
   A long blow up the back and then you turn, turn around.

   Chorus

"Widegoara Joe" is an education in the art of sheep shearing, including the names of some Australian "immortals" of that era—that is, in the opinion of the backblock shearer.

Widgegoara Joe

WIDGEGOARA JOE
(The Backblock Shearer)

1. I'm only a backblock shearer, as easily can be seen;
   I've shore in almost every shed in the plains of Riverine.
   I've shore in most of the famous sheds, I've seen big tallies done,
   But somehow or other, I don't know why, I never became a gun.

   Chorus
   Hurrah my boys, my shears are set, I feel both fit and well.
   Tomorrow will find me at my pen, when the gaffer rings the bell.
   With Haydon's patent thumb-guards fixed, and both my blades
       pulled back,
   Tomorrow I go with my siding blow for a century or the sack.

2. I've opened up the windpipe straight; I've opened behind
       the ear;
   I've practiced every possible style in which a man can shear;
   I've studied all the cuts and drives of the famous men I've met,
   But I never succeeded in plastering up those three little figures
       yet.

   Chorus

3. As the boss walked down this morning, I saw him stare at me,
   For I'd mastered Moran's great shoulder-cut, as he could plainly
       see.
   But I've another surprise for him that'll give his nerves a shock,
   Tomorrow he'll find that I have mastered Pierce's rang-tang
       block.

   Chorus

4. If I succeed, as I hope to do, then I intend to shear
   At the Wagga demonstration which is held there every year!
   And there I'll lower the colours, the colours of Mitchell and Co.,
   Instead of Deeming you will hear of Widgegoara Joe!

   Chorus

Sheep-washing in Queensland — Illustrated London News, 13th of August, 1865.

This is the story, in song, of "The Sheepwasher," who had experienced good times in the past, bad times in the present, and is hoping for a future when "cringing poverty is driven from our land."

THE SHEEPWASHER

THE SHEEPWASHER

1. When first I took the Western track, 'twas many years ago,
   No master then stood up so high, no servant stood so low;
   But now the squatters, puffed with pride, do treat us with disdain.
   Lament with me the bygone days that will not come again.

2. I had a pair of ponies once, to bear me on the road.
   I earned a decent cheque at times, and blued it like a lord.
   But lonely now I hump my drum, in sunshine and in rain,
   Lamenting on the bygone days that will not come again.

3. Let bushmen all in unity combine with heart and hand
   'Til bloody cringing poverty is driven from our land.
   Let never Queensland come to know the tyrant's ball and chain,
   And workers all in time to come their vanished rights regain.

"The Ram of Dalby," a tall tale of the Australian sheep with their incomparable wool, is easily traceable to the English, "The Ram of Derby." Originating in Queensland, some versions of the chorus revert to the use of "Derby" instead of "Dalby."

The Ram Of Dalby

THE RAM OF DALBY

1. As I went to Dalby, upon a market day,
   I saw the finest sheep there was ever fed on hay.

   Chorus
   Aye wrinkle Dalby, Dalby wrinkle day,
   Wrinkle wrinkle Dalby, for Dalby can today.

2. The wool grew on his belly, it grew into the ground;
   Cut off and sent to Dalby, it fetched a thousand pound.

   Chorus

3. The wool grew on his backbone, the wool grew up so high
   A hawk had built her nest there, I heard the young ones cry.

   Chorus

4. The wool grew on his shoulders, it grew up to the moon;
   A man went up in September, and never came down till June.

   Chorus

5. The man who raised this sheep up, he must be mighty rich.
   The man who made this song up is a lying son of the West!

   Chorus

"The Banks of the Condamine," a dialogue ballad, is related to all such songs in which the girl offers to disguise herself as a man, to accompany her lover whether aboard ship, on the battlefield or whatever the circumstances may be. Nancy is willing to play a less romantic role: to "wash his greasy moleskins."

THE BANKS OF THE CONDAMINE

In narrative style

THE BANKS OF THE CONDAMINE

1. Man:　O hark, the dogs are barking, love, I can no longer stay.
The men are all gone mustering, and it is nearly day.
And I must be off by morning light
　　before the sun does shine,
To meet the Roma shearers on the banks
　　of the Condamine.

2. Girl:　O Willy, dearest Willy, O let me go with you!
I'll cut off my auburn fringe and be a shearer too.
I'll cook and count your tally, love, while ringer—
　　O you shine,
And I'll wash your greasy moleskins on the banks
　　of the Condamine.

3. Man:　O Nancy, dearest Nancy, with me you cannot go!
The squatters have given orders, love,
　　no woman should do so.
And your delicate condition is not equal unto mine,
To withstand the constant tigering on the banks
　　of the Condamine.

4. Girl:　O Willy, dearest Willy, then stay at home with me.
We'll take up a selection, and a farmer's wife I'll be.
I'll help you husk the corn, love,
　　and cook your meals so fine.
You'll forget the ram-stag mutton on the banks
　　of the Condamine.

5. Man:　O Nancy, dearest Nancy, pray do not hold me back!
Down there the boys are waiting,
　　and I must be on the track.
So here's a goodbye kiss, love: back home I will incline
When we've shore the last of the jumbucks on the banks
　　of the Condamine.

Of the humorous songs of the pioneer life in the Australian bush, "The Old Bark Hut" is one of the most popular. The United States cowboy counterpart is "The Little Old Log Shanty on the Plain."

"I'm looking rather seedy now while holding down my claim,
And my victuals are not always served the best;
And the mice play shyly round me as I nestle down to rest
In my little old log shanty on the plain."

With words in the same vein is "The Alberta Homesteader," of Canadian folklore, usually sung to "The Irish Washerwoman." This tells of Dan Gold as he gets into bed while:

"The rattlesnake rattles a tune at my head,
The little mosquito devoid of all fear
Crawls over my face and into my ear."

THE OLD BARK HUT

ONCE WAS WELL TO DO, MY LADS, BUT NOW I'M SO HARD UP, THAT I'M
FORCED TO GO ON RA-TIONS IN AN OLD BARK HUT. IN AN
OLD BARK HUT, IN AN OLD BARK HUT, THAT I'M
FORCED TO GO ON RA-TIONS IN AN OLD BARK HUT.
CHORUS

THE OLD BARK HUT

1. Oh, my name is Bob the swagman and I'll have you understand,
   I've seen a lot of ups and downs while trav'ling through the land.
   I once was well to do, my lads, but now I'm so hard up
   That I'm forced to go on rations in an old bark hut.

   Chorus
   In an old bark hut, in an old bark hut,
   (REPEAT THE LAST LINE OF EACH STANZA.)

2. Ten pounds of flour, ten pounds of beef, some sugar and some tay,
   That's all they give a hungry man until the seventh day.
   If you don't be mighty sparing, you go with a hungry gut.
   That's one of the great misfortunes of an old bark hut!

   Chorus

3. The bucket I wash me feet in has to cook me tay and stew.
   They'd say I was getting mighty flash if I should ask for two.
   The table's just a sheet of bark—goodness knows when it was cut!
   It was blown from the rafters of the old bark hut.

   Chorus

4. I've had the rain come pouring in just like a perfect flood,
   Especially through the great big hole where once the table stood.
   It leaves me not a single spot where I can lay me nut,
   But the rain is sure to find me in the old bark hut.

   Chorus

5. Beside the fire I lay me down, wrapped up in two old rugs.
   You couldn't call it comfort, but it seems to lure the bugs!
   And all I've got for company's the poor old collie slut,
   So I use her for a pillow in the old bark hut.

   Chorus

6. So now I've sung me little song as nicely as I could.
   I hope the ladies present will not think my language rude.
   And all you handsome girls and boys, around me growing up,
   Remember Bob the swagman in his old bark hut.

Chorus

The words of "The Dying Stockman" are reminiscent of "O Bury Me Not on the Lone Prairie," of western United States cowboy origin.

"O bury me not on the lone prairie,
Where the coyotes howl and the wind blows free."

One may also be reminded of the Canadian ballad, "The Dying Outlaw," of the same era. His request was the opposite of the cowboy as he sings:

"O bury me on the lone prairie,
Where the hooves of the horses shall fall."

* The Dying Stockman

*Effective if sung a capella (unaccompanied) by a quartet of mixed voices.

THE DYING STOCKMAN

1. A strapping young stockman lay dying,
   A saddle supporting his head.
   And his comrades around him were crying,
   As he leant on his elbow and said:

   Chorus
   "Wrap me up in my stockwhip and blanket
   And bury me deep down below,
   Where the dingoes and crows will not find me,
   In the shade where the coolibahs grow.

2. Cut down a couple of saplings,
   Place one at my head and my toe.
   Carve on them a stockwhip and saddle
   To show there's a stockman below.

   Chorus

3. There's some tea in that battered old billy;
   Place the pannikins all in a row.
   And we'll drink to the next merry meeting,
   In the place where all good stockmen go.

   Chorus

4. I hear the wail of a dingo
   In the gloom of the scrubs down below.
   And he rings the knell of a stockman.
   Farewell, dear old pals, I must go.

   Chorus

5. If I had the wings of a pigeon,
   Far over the plains I would fly.
   I'd fly to the arms of my loved ones,
   And there I would lay down and die."

   Chorus

Products from the outback had to be transported to market. Pack horses in the earliest days were the only means of transportation. Later, for long and heavy hauls, bullock wagons were the improved method of conveying goods from place to place.

"Bullocky—O" has a nameless driver, but one full of vim and vigor as he boasts of his accomplishments.

BULLOCKY - O

WING; I'M THE KING OF BULL-OCK DRIV-ERS, DON'T YOU
KNOW, BULL-OCK-Y —— O! I'M THE KING OF BULL-OCK
CHORUS
DRIV—ERS, DON'T YOU KNOW, BULL-OCK—Y —— O!
D7
G
D7
G
C
G

BULLOCKY—O

1. I draw for Speckle's mill, bullocky—O, bullocky—O,
   And it's many a log I drew, bullocky—O.
   I draw cedar, beech and pine, and I never get on the wine;
   I'm the King of bullock drivers, don't you know, bullocky—O!

   Chorus
   I'm the King of bullock drivers, don't you know, bullocky—O!

2. There's Guinea and Anderson too, bullocky—O, bullocky—O!
   And it's many a log they drew, bullocky—O.
   I can give 'em a thousand feet, axe 'em square and never cheat,
   I'm the King of bullock drivers, don't you know, bullocky—O!

   Chorus

3. There's Wapples, too, he brags, bullocky—O, bullocky—O,
   Of his forty rawboned stags, bullocky—O.
   I can tell you it's no slander when I say I raise their dander,
   When they hear the crack of me whip, bullocky—O, bullocky—O!

   Chorus

A team of perhaps eight or ten bullocks might be necessary for a long or heavy haul; if large enough, two bullockies or drivers would be hired. When the mileage was great or the weather did not cooperate, it could take months for the journey. Rains could make the roads impassable for weeks at a time. When the team returned home with supplies to last until the next trip, the event can well be imagined.

Whether on a long or short haul, the bullockies were always a welcome sight to the stranded residents of the bush. They brought not only needed stores but news and tales of the countryside.

"Bill, the Bullocky" was such a person.

Bill, the Bullocky

BILL, THE BULLOCKY

1. As I came down through Conroy's Gap,
   I heard a maiden cry,
   "There goes old Bill, the Bullocky;
   He's bound for Gundagai.
   A better bullock driver never
   Cracked an honest crust;
   A kinder hearted driver never dragged a whip through dust."

2. His team got bogged at Five Mile Creek;
   Bill lashed and cried and swore:
   "If Nobby don't haul us out of this
   I'll speak to him no more!"
   So Nobby strained and broke the yoke,
   And poked out Baldy's eye,
   And the dog sat on the tucker box
   Five miles from Gundagai.

Making their contribution to the folklore of the bush were the drovers, another of the nomad trades. Sung after a successful trip, rather than during it, are the songs asserting the superiority of the drovers, particularly the Queensland overlanders.

THE QUEENSLAND DROVER

THE QUEENSLAND DROVER

1. There's a trade you all know well,
   It's bringing cattle over.
   On ev'ry track, to the Gulf and back,
   Men know the Queensland drover.

   Chorus
   Pass the billy round, my boys!
   Don't let the pint-pot stand there!
   For tonight we drink the health of ev'ry overlander.

2. I come from the northern plains,
   Where the girls and the grass are scanty,
   Where the creeks run dry or ten foot high,
   And it's either drought or plenty.

   Chorus

3. There are men from ev'ry land,
   From Spain and France and Flanders;
   They're a well-mixed pack, two races here,
   The Queensland overlanders.

   Chorus

4. As I pass along the roads,
   The children raise my dander,
   Crying: "Mother, dear, take in the clothes,
   Here comes an overlander!"

   Chorus

5. Now I'm bound for home once more,
   On a prad that's guite a goer;
   I can find a job with a crawling mob
   On the banks of the Maranoa.

   Chorus

Riding round their cattle at night, they sang ballads to which any number of verses were added, soothing the restless cattle and hopefully keeping the drover awake.

THE DROVER'S DREAM

THE DROVER'S DREAM

1. One night, when trav'ling sheep, my companions lay asleep,
   There was not a star to 'luminate the sky.
   I was dreaming, I suppose, for my eyes were partly closed,
   When a very strange procession passed me by.
   First there came a kangaroo with his swag of blankets blue,
   A dingo ran beside him as his mate;
   They were trav'ling mighty fast, but they shouted as they passed,
   "We'll have to jog along; it's getting late."

2. The pelican and the crane, they came in from off the plain
   To amuse the company with a Highland Fling.
   The dear old bandicoot played the tune upon his flute,
   And the native bears sat round them in a ring.
   The drongo and the crow sang us songs of long ago,
   The frill-necked lizard listened with a smile;
   And the emu, standing near, with his claw up to his ear
   Said: "Funniest thing I've heard for quite a while."

3. The frogs from out the swamp, where the atmosphere is damp,
   Came bounding in and sat upon the stones.
   They each unrolled their swags, and produced from little bags
   The violin, the banjo and the bones.
   The goanna and the snake and the adder, wide awake,
   With an alligator danced "The Soldier's Joy,"
   In the spreading silky-oak the jackass cracked a joke,
   And the magpie sang "The Wild Colonial Boy."

4. Some brolgas darted out from the tea-tree all about,
   And performed a set of Lancers very well.
   Then the parrot green and blue gave the orchestra its cue
   To strike up "The Old Log Cabin in the Dell."
   I was dreaming, I suppose, of these entertaining shows,
   But it never crossed my mind I was asleep,
   Till the boss, beneath the cart, woke me up with such a start
   Yelling: "Dreamy, where the heck are all the sheep?"

Ladies Of Brisbane

After the long, lonely trek overlanding the cattle, the drovers relaxed with music and dancing in the company of the "Ladies of Brisbane," before returning to the "old cattle station."

There are several versions of this song, with words varying according to the location. This one relates to the Queensland drovers and is the original parody of "Spanish Ladies," an old English sea song.

LADIES OF BRISBANE

1. Farewell and adieu to you, Brisbane Ladies.
   Farewell and adieu to the girls of Toowong.
   We have sold all our cattle and cannot now linger,
   But we hope we shall see you again before long.

   Chorus
   For we rant and we roar like true Queensland natives,
   We rant and we roar as onward we push,
   Until we return to the old cattle station,
   What joy and delight is the life in the bush!

2. The first camp we make is called the Quart-pot,
   Caboolture and Kilcoy, then Colinton hut;
   We pull up at Stonehouse, Bob Williams' paddock,
   And early next morning we cross the Blackbutt.

   Chorus

3. On, on! past Taromeo to Yarraman Creek, boys!
   It's there where we'll make a fine camp for the day.
   Where the water and grass are both plenty and good, boys,
   The life of a drover is merry and gay.

   Chorus

4. Now the camp is all snug and supper is over,
   We sit round the fire enjoying a smoke
   And yarning of dog and of cattle and horses,
   'Til all join in chorus to "Grandfather's Clock."

Chorus

5. Then it's right through Nanango, that jolly old township,
   "Good day to you lads," with a hearty shake-hands;
   "Come on, this is my shout!" "Well, here's to our next trip."
   "And we hope you'll come back, boys, tonight to our dance."

Chorus

6. Oh, the girls look so pretty; the sight is entrancing;
   Bewitching and graceful they join in the fun,
   The waltz, polka, first step and all other dancing
   To the old concertina of Jack Smith the Don.

Chorus

TWENTIETH CENTURY AUSTRALIA

Federation—The Commonwealth of Australia

World Wars I and II
  "Waltzing Matilda"

Holidays
  New Year's Day, Australian Day, Good Friday,
  Easter, Anzac Day, Queen's Birthday,
  Labour or Eight Hour Day, Boxing Day

Christmas
  "The Three Drovers"
  "Carol of the Birds"
  "An Australian Christmas Carol"
  "The Twelve Days of Christmas"

The Aborigines Today
  "Djerag—The Shark"
  "The Honey Ant Song of Ljaba"

Modern Australian history begins with federation. By the end of the nineteenth century, the colonies realized that their internal and external defence and their economic advancement could never be achieved by six separate and self governing colonies. The Australian democracy chose its own men, the majority of whom were native born, to meet in intercolonial conferences to frame its new constitution. Under an Act of the British Parliament, the Commonwealth of Australia came into being on January 1, 1901, the six colonies becoming states. Melbourne was the capital until Canberra, the newly selected site, was ready in the 1920's.

A little more than a decade later, on August 14, 1914, telegraph messages were sent from London to all parts of the British dominions, informing them that a state of war existed with the German Empire. The Commonwealth of Australia pledged itself to prosecute the war on land and sea with the utmost vigor. This was no small task for a country that had never been involved in any warfare whether internal or external. Men were e listed, put into uniform, equipped, trained and then transported 12,000 miles to the theater of war. The Australian and New Zealand Army Corps, from which came the name Anzac, distinguished themselves in all spheres of operation.

By 1939, when Britain again declared war on Germany, all Australian political parties united in support of Britain. Pro-British and anti-Nazi sentiment was strong. Fortunately, there were two factors favorable to Australia in preparing for a major conflict which eventually was to come too close to her home shores for comfort: this was the period of the "phony" war in Europe and Japan had not yet entered World War II.

After the entry of the Japanese into the conflict, it was soon apparent that the major role of Australia was to be the supply center for the Pacific War effort. Whether as the "arsenal of the Pacific" or as the "bread basket" for the Allied Forces, whether performing on the industrial or war fronts, the Australians discharged their duties with valor and distinction.

As the Pacific war gathered momentum, Australia was in immediate and grave danger. No direct help could be anticipated from Britain, to whom they had always looked for defence. Japan was acknowledged to be a first class military power and the Australian forces were known to be totally inadequate to defend the home front. In a New Year's declaration, Prime Minister John Curtin stated at the time of the Japanese advances throughout Asia: "Without inhibition of any kind, I make it quite clear that Australia looks to America, free of any pangs as to our traditional links or kinship with the United Kingdom." The ties that had bound Australia to England for over a century and a half were finally and publicly severed and Australia emerged from the war as a sovereign nation able to stand on its own.

It was during World Wars I and II that the best known of Australia's traditional music sang its way around the world. Later the ceremonies of the Olympic Games in Melbourne in 1956 gave an added impetus to an already sky-rocketing song.

It seems incredible that a simple, rollicking ballad such as "Waltzing Matilda" should have been, and continues to be, the cause of a great deal of controversy; several books have been written on the subject. The conflicting theories as to its origin are due to the fact that, until recent times, the Australian archives have been in a deplorable, if not an almost non-existent state. It is well nigh impossible to shed much light on the subject historically from that source.

The song originated, it is believed, in Queensland about 1898. After achieving a certain amount of popularity in that region, a Sydney firm of tea merchants called Inglis in 1906 appropriated the song, giving free copies of it with their "Billy" brand of tea. The following year, it was included in the "Australian Student's Song Book," which was used extensively throughout Australia. Copyrighted in 1936, the increasingly popular ballad was printed as a separate number by an Australian publisher.

About this time, a visiting Englishman, on his return to England, included "Waltzing Matilda" in a book describing his Australian experiences, calling it the only authentic Australian folk song he had encountered there. Published by Oxford University Press, affairs became entangled temporarily with the Australian publisher of the song, detracting not at all from the further promotion of the ballad.

The examination of the several varying editions of the song raises many questions by interested students of the subject. It is still unresolved whether the melody can be traced to the Scotch tune "Craigielea" or to a seventeenth century British military march, "The Bold Fusilier," whether composed by Christina Macpherson, Harry Nathan or Marie Cowan. The words are attributed to A. B. Paterson, one of Australia's most popular poets of that era.

"Waltzing Matilda" today is called by some "The Unofficial National Anthem of Australia," while others are fiercely challenging the idea. So the controversy about the simple and most popular ballad of the people "Down Under" continues unabated.

Waltzing Matilda

Words by A.B.Paterson

Music by Marie Cowan
Arr. by Orrie Lee

With an easy swing – lightly and gaily

Eb　Bbdim.　C7　Fm7　Bb7　Eb
"You'll come a - waltz - ing ma — til — da with me!"
"You'll come a - waltz - ing ma — til — da with me!"
Chorus
Eb　Eb7　Ab　Fmi7　Ebdim.　Eb　Fmi7　Eb
Waltz-ing ma-til-da, waltz-ing ma-til-da, you'll come a-waltz-ing ma-
Fmi7　Bb7　Eb　Bb7　Fdim.
- til - da with me. And he sang as he watched and stowed that
Cm　Fm　Fmi7　Eb　C7　Fmi7　Bb7　Eb
Wait-ed till his bil-ly boiled. "You'll come a-waltz-ing ma - til-da with me!"
Jum-buck in his tuck-er bag.
Repeat for 2nd Verse

3. UP RODE THE SQUAT — TER, MOUNT — ED ON HIS THOR-OUGH-BRED,
4. UP JUMPED THE SWAG — MAN, SPRANG IN — TO THE BIL — LA — BONG.
DOWN CAME THE TROOP — ERS, ONE, TWO, THREE:
"YOU'LL NEV — ER CATCH ME A — LIVE," SAID HE. AND HIS
"WHERE'S THAT JOL — LY JUM — BUCK YOU'VE GOT IN YOUR TUCK — ER BAG?"
GHOST MAY BE HEARD AS YOU PASS — BY THAT BIL — LA — BONG,
"YOU'LL COME A — WALTZ — ING MA — TIL — DA WITH ME!"
"YOU'LL COME A — WALTZ — ING MA — TIL — DA WITH ME!"

CHORUS
WALTZ-ING MA-TIL-DA, WALTZ-ING MA-TIL-DA,
YOU'LL COME A-WALTZ-ING MA-TIL-DA WITH ME. AND HIS
"WHERE'S THAT JOL-LY JUM-BUCK YOU'VE GOT IN YOUR TUCK-ER BAG?"
GHOST MAY BE HEARD AS YOU PASS BY THAT BIL-LA-BONG,
"YOU'LL COME A-WALTZ-ING MA-TIL-DA WITH ME!"
-TIL-DA WITH ME!"
D.S. for 4th verse, after which
Chorus repeats ad lib.

HOLIDAYS

In most countries throughout the world, holidays and festivals are and have been an integral and anticipated part of their culture; Australia is no exception. In each of the states and territories comprising the Commonwealth of Australia, some holidays may be added or deleted from the national roster. However, the well established celebrations throughout the land are:

New Year's Day—January 1

Australia Day—January 26—commemorates the first settlement at Sydney Cove, under the leadership of Governor Arthur Phillip, on January 26, 1788.

Good Friday and *Easter* are observed in March or April as designated by the Christian world.

**Anzac Day*—April 25— honors the Australian and New Zealand Army Corps (Anzacs) who, on that day, landed at Gallipoli during World War I, fought heroically for months, suffered heavy casualties and eventual defeat in one of the most poorly planned military campaigns of the war.

The Queen's Birthday varies, as in England, with the date determined each year.

Labour or Eight Hour Day occurs in the fall or spring.

Christmas—December 25

Boxing Day—December 26—in name, at least, is a relic of sixteenth century England, when, on the day after Christmas, servants and apprentices, carrying boxes with a slit in the lid, visited their masters, soliciting gifts of money. This custom has long since died, but the day, retaining its name, has continued as a holiday for sports or whatever relaxation is most enjoyed.

Those holidays that are not religious in nature feature picnics, (weather permitting), sports events according to the season, parades to the strains of American and European band music, and the playing and singing of old traditional songs, including, of course, "Waltzing Matilda."

---

*Australia is the only country that celebrates a defeat on the battlefield.

CHRISTMAS

Whether the celebrants are Old or New Australians, Christmas was and is observed traditionally by them as in the homeland, with carols, gifts, greeting cards, church attendance and family home-comings for the festivities. Because of the hot December days, there are those who are breaking away from a table laden with the heavy food of Christmas as in the Northern Hemisphere and are serving the more sensible summer fare of salads, a picnic spread at home, the beach or the countryside.

Musically, however, they adhere to custom, so that the beloved carols of England and other European countries are those most generally sung.

Gaining in popularity, particularly with the younger people, are some carols peculiar to Down Under, composed in a traditional style, with texts more appropriate to a hot December climate and to their own particular culture. Hopefully this should continue also in the popular field. It is only wishful thinking or a resort to memories that would prompt one to sing in Australia of the Yule log, "A White Christmas," "Winter Wonderland," "Chestnuts roasting on an open fire, Jack Frost nipping at your nose," or of "Dashing through the snow, in a one horse open sleigh."

William G. James, for many years the Australian Broadcasting Commission's first Federal Controller of Music, has contributed to Australian music literature as composer of vocal and extended orchestral works. But perhaps he will be best remembered as composer of a group of Christmas carols that, with their lilting melodies and rhythms, set to simple words by John Wheeler, have already become an integral part of the Australian Christmas season.

Why not sing of "The Three Drovers" instead of, or in addition to "The Three Wise Men"?

The Three Drovers

Words by JOHN WHEELER   Music by WILLIAM G. JAMES

Printed by permission of the copyright owner, Chappell and Co., Ltd., 68 Clarence Street, Sydney, Australia.

THE THREE DROVERS

1. Across the plains one Christmas night,
   Three drovers riding blythe and gay,
   Looked up and saw a starry light,
   More radiant than the Milky Way;
   And on their hearts such wonder fell,
   They sang with joy "Noel! Noel!
   Noel! Noel! Noel!"

2. The air was dry with summer heat,
   and smoke was on the yellow moon;
   But from the Heavens, faint and sweet,
   came floating down a wond'rous tune;
   And, as they heard, they sang full well,
   those drovers three—"Noel! Noel!
   Noel! Noel! Noel!"

3. The black swans flew across the sky,
   The wild dog called across the plain,
   The starry lustre blazed on high,
   Still echoed on the Heavenly strain;
   And still they sang "Noel! Noel!"
   Those drovers three. "Noel! Noel!
   Noel! Noel! Noel!"

Brolgas, woodlarks, friar birds, bell birds, currawongs and lorikeets make this a uniquely Australian "Carol of the Birds," appropriately concluding with an aboriginal greeting to Christmas Day.

CAROL OF THE BIRDS

Words by JOHN WHEELER   Music by WILLIAM G. JAMES

Printed by permission of the copyright owner, Chappell and Co., Ltd., 68 Clarence Street, Sydney, Australia.

CAROL OF THE BIRDS

1. Out on the plains the brolgas are dancing
   Lifting their feet like warhorses prancing:
   Up to the sun the woodlarks go winging
   Faint in the dawn—light echoes their singing
   "Orana! Orana! Orana! to Christmas Day!"

2. Down where the tree-ferns grow by the river,
   There where the waters sparkle and quiver,
   Deep in the gullies bell-birds are chiming,
   Softly and sweetly their lyric notes rhyming—
   "Orana! Orana! Orana! to Christmas Day!"

3. Friar-birds sip the nectar of flowers,
   Currawongs chant in wattle-tree bowers;
   In the blue ranges lorikeets calling—
   Carols of bushbirds rising and falling—
   "Orana! Orana! Orana! to Christmas Day!"

"An Australian Christmas Carol" is in the more formal style of an anthem, available as a solo, duet or quartet for mixed voices. The old Irish traditional melody is arranged by Dr. Percy Jones, composer and vice director of the Conservatorium of Music in the University of Melbourne.

The text is by a nun, a member of the Order of Loreto Sisters (Institutio Beatae Mariae Virginia) who, instead of using her name, substitutes the initials of the order to which she belongs.

An Australian Christmas Carol
TWO-PART ANTHEM

Words by I.B.V.M.

Music arr. by
PERCY JONES
(After an ancient Irish tune)

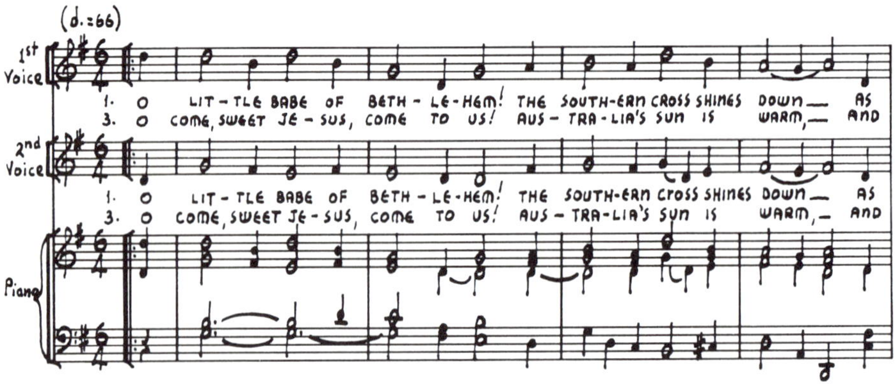

Printed by permission of the copyright owner, Allan and Co., Pty. Ltd., 276 Collins Street, Melbourne, Australia.

AN AUSTRALIAN CHRISTMAS CAROL

1. O little Babe of Bethlehem!
   The Southern Cross shines down—
   As once a star shone glorious
   Above an eastern town.

2. The hearts of Bethlehem are cold,
   The streets are hushed with snow,
   The doors are barred, there is no room,
   Dear Lord, where wilt Thou go?

3. O come, sweet Jesus, come to us!
   Australia's sun is warm,
   And here are loving hearts enough
   To shield Thee from the storm.

4. Come! we will give Thee all we have,
   Each bird, and flower and tree,
   The breeze that stirs the silver gums,
   The music of the sea.

5. And sweet wild clematis starry-eyed,
   With delicate ferns we'll bring;
   Our wattle trees shall shower their gold
   In tribute to our King.

6. We'll watch, when evening sounds begin,
   And dreaming flowers nod,
   Thy Mother fold Thee in her arms,
   Thou little Lamb of God.

7. Bell-birds shall ring their silver peal
   From gullies green and deep,
   And mingle with the magpies' note
   To call Thee from Thy sleep.

8. O little Babe of Bethlehem
   Australia loves Thee well,
   Come to our hearts this Christmastide,
   And there forever dwell.

Fun to sing is the old English cumulative carol, "The Twelve Days of Christmas," creating words that relate to the fauna and flora of Australia, in place of "A Partridge in a Pear Tree."

TWO STATE-LY BROL-GAS AND A KOOK-A-BUR-RA IN A GUM TREE.
No repeat for stanza 3.
3. ON THE THIRD DAY OF CHRIST-MAS MY TRUE LOVE GAVE TO ME, 3. THREE WOOL-Y JUM-BUCKS
4. ON THE FOURTH DAY OF CHRIST-MAS MY TRUE LOVE GAVE TO ME, 4. FOUR DANC-ING SHEI-LAS, THREE WOOL-Y JUM-BUCKS
TWO STATE-LY BROL-GAS AND A KOOK-A-BUR-RA IN A GUM TREE.
Broadly
5. ON THE FIFTH DAY OF CHRIST-MAS MY TRUE LOVE GAVE TO ME, FIVE O-PAL
Broadly
A tempo
RINGS, FOUR DANC-ING SHEI-LAS, THREE WOOL-Y JUM-BUCKS, TWO STATE-LY BROL-GAS AND A
A tempo

KOOK-A-BUR-RA IN A GUM TREE.
6. ON THE SIXTH DAY OF CHRIST-MAS MY
7. ON THE SEVENTH DAY OF CHRIST-MAS MY
8. ON THE EIGHTH DAY OF CHRIST-MAS MY
(Continue 9th, 10th, 11th, 12th day)
(No repeat for stanza 6. Repeat as many times as necessary for succeeding stanzas.)
TRUE LOVE GAVE TO ME;
TRUE LOVE GAVE TO ME;
6. SIX JUMP-ING KAN-GA-ROOS,
7. SEVEN CUTE KO—A-LA BEARS,
SIX JUMP-ING KAN-GA-ROOS,
8. EIGHT EMP-TY TUCK-ER BAGS,
SEVEN CUTE KO—A-LA BEARS,
SIX JUMP-ING KAN-GA-ROOS,
Broadly
FIVE O-PAL RINGS,
A tempo
FOUR DANC-ING SHEI-LAS
THREE WOOL-Y JUM-BUCKS
Broadly
A tempo
TWO STATE-LY BROL-GAS, AND A KOOK-A-BUR-RA IN A GUM TREE.

THE TWELVE DAYS OF CHRISTMAS

1. On the first day of Christmas my true love gave to me,
   A kookaburra in a gum tree.

2. On the second day of Christmas my true love gave to me,
   Two stately brolgas and a kookaburra in a gum tree.

3. On the third day of Christmas my true love gave to me,
   Three wooly jumbucks, two stately brolgas and a kookaburra
      in a gum tree.

4. On the fourth day of Christmas my true love gave to me,
   Four dancing sheilas, three wooly jumbucks, etc.

5. On the fifth day of Christmas my true love gave to me,
   Five opal rings, four dancing sheilas, three wooly jumbucks, etc.

6. On the sixth day of Christmas my true love gave to me,
   Six jumping kangaroos, five opal rings, four dancing sheilas, etc.

7. On the seventh day of Christmas my true love gave to me,
   Seven cute koala bears, six jumping kangaroos, five opal rings, etc.

8. On the eighth day of Christmas my true love gave to me,
   Eight empty tucker bags, seven cute koala bears, etc.

9. On the ninth day of Christmas my true love gave to me,
   Nine tennis rackets, eight empty tucker bags, etc.

10. On the tenth day of Christmas my true love gave to me,
    Ten prancing neddies, nine tennis rackets, etc.

11. On the eleventh day of Christmas my true love gave to me,
    Eleven tin billies, ten prancing neddies, etc.

12. On the twelfth day of Christmas my true love gave to me,
    Twelve crested bellbirds, eleven tin billies, etc.

THE ABORIGINES TODAY

For centuries unnumbered these brown-skinned aborigines occupied a most inhospitable land as to soil, climate and available resources. They made the necessary and not too easy adaptations and survived, evolving a highly complex primitive society.

From the advent of the white man in 1788 until the present time, the adjustment of the aborigine to the white man, and the white man to the aborigine, has been difficult and not always successful. Many attempts have been made toward a better understanding; different avenues of approach have been undertaken; trial and error has been the usual performance.

The aborigines numbered about 500,000 when the English first came to Australia. Today there are approximately 40,000 purebloods and an equal number of mixed-bloods. The former are chiefly to be found in the far north, in Arnhem Land, where the old way of aboriginal life continues to survive. Some of the detribalized aborigines live on Government and "mission" stations, supported by Government grants. Others have found occupations as miners, laborers, stockmen on cattle stations, in factories or domestic service. Recently, many of the mixed-bloods have settled in the cities.

Place names on the continent and some 150 words in the Australian vocabulary show the aboriginal influence. Lately the Australian Institute of Aboriginal Studies in Canberra, and Chairs of Aboriginal Anthropology at leading universities are concerned with recording and preserving the ancient culture of these peoples before it is too late.

Sporadic research studies of the aborigines were made in the nineteenth century. However, it is since World War II that the anthropologists and ethno-musicologists, using the latest in recording devices, have had, in every sense of the word, a "field day." Particularly is this true in Arnhem Land, where A. P. Elkin and Trevor Jones have investigated, recorded and analyzed, to a remarkable degree of thoroughness, every aspect of the daily living of certain tribes. Arnhem Land, for those interested in locating it on the map, includes part of the northern peninsula in the Northern Territory, some two hundred miles east of Darwin and north of the Roper River.

What is true in Arnhem Land may or may not apply to other tribes sparsely scattered across the continent. Musically there may be distinct differences in rhythmic structure, in the instruments used in the singing and dancing, in the vocal quality of the singers or in the types of scales forming the melodies.

Each tribe or totem has its Headman, most carefully selected and trained and with the greatest authority. Next in importance is the Songman, chosen at an early age. He, first of all, must be one who has been initiated into the tribe (a long, painful and exhausting trial of strength and endurance, which only the fittest, mentally and physically, are able to bear). In addition, he must be endowed with an excellent singing voice along with other musical abilities; memory is essential for the memorizing of legends which have been passed down orally from generation to generation; psychic powers are necessary as he learns songs in dreams from the spirits of the dead. It is he who teaches these ancient chants to the younger, incoming Songman.

Like the Songman, the didjeridoo player is carefully selected and, when chosen, devotes his life to this profession. Beginning his training at an early age, a good player or "puller" may become a celebrity, not only in his own clan, but throughout the district.

The didjeridoo, a crude wind instrument, is without a known parallel in primitive music. A hollow tube of bamboo or other wood, it is five or six feet in length, about three inches in diameter, and sometimes fitted with a mouthpiece of wood or clay. With no reed or other sound producing device, it simply acts as a resonating pipe into which the player blows, his lips vibrating as in a trombone or tuba.

In performance, a drone on a low note (between a D flat and G below the bass clef) is broken up into any number of rhythmic patterns and accents by the skillful manipulation of tongue and cheeks. The most skilled didjeridoo performer, in addition, may use two different notes, alternated in rapid succession as the rhythm pattern becomes quite complex. The two notes are usually pitched a major tenth apart, with the high note being blown very lightly to give the effect of a drum. A performance of this skill must be heard to be appreciated.

If the aborigines have not developed the large range of instruments used by some primitive peoples, they have evolved, for their own use in Arnhem Land, a seemingly simple instrument to infinite possibilities.

The didjeridoo is used to accompany only secular music. In all aboriginal chants, secular or sacred, each singer accompanies himself with sticks. These are cylindrical, made of hard, resonant wood which, when struck together, sound almost metallic. Used in pairs, they are twelve to fifteen inches long and about one inch in diameter. It is only in secular music that the players of the sticks become quite adventurous by remaining silent for one or two beats while the didjeridoo carries on.

In place of sticks, a pair (or pairs) of boomerangs are used in certain ceremonies. In other rites, dancers may strike their hand or the ground with a bark pad.

Since time immemorial, the simplest form of marking rhythm is practiced by these people: handclapping by onlookers and participants, or the striking of thighs or other parts of the body with cupped hands.

This Djerag, a tribal song from northeast Arnhem Land, is performed and enjoyed around the campfire. It is just one of many Djerags, whose subjects treat of birds found in coastal regions, or the inhabitants of the sea.

"The Shark (Marauwa)" tells its own story in the aboriginal language of the performers. Freely translated into English, it is accompanied by some creative stick players and a swinging didjeridoo "puller."

An instrumental prelude by the sticks or didjeridoo always introduces the singers. The final measure of two notes is a solo by the Songman. Unaccompanied by instruments, this recitative is performed in free rhythm, with the two notes alternating irregularly.

DJERAG — THE SHARK (MARAUWA)

Ljába, an area of the Aranda speaking section of Central Australia, was the chief honey-ant center for that region. The honey-ant, an unusual insect, lived under the roots of the mulga tree. Intentionally overfed by the workers of the ant colony, its abdomen became so distended with honey that it eventually could not move. Instead of supplying its own ant colony with food, it was gathered daily by the Aranda women to add to their often meager diet.

The words, in couplets, are repeated over and over again to form ever lengthening verses; some versions of the song have seventeen such verses. The Arandans are chanting, not only about ordinary honey-ants (verses 1, 4, 5), but identifying with them as their an-

cestors while imaginatively decorating parts of their bodies with
down, paint and cob-webs (verses 2, 3).

Honey Ant Song Of Lja'ba (Makerenben)

(English Translation)

1. The ant workers yonder dwell, ever dwell.
   In ring-tiered homes they dwell, ever dwell.

2. With down-hooded heads they dwell, ever dwell.
   With stripe-banded chests they dwell, ever dwell.

3. With cob-webbed closed eyes they dwell, ever dwell.
   With down-hooded heads they dwell, ever dwell.

4. In cellared cells they dwell, ever dwell.
   With bodies ring-rimmed they dwell, ever dwell.

5. In cellared cells they dwell, ever dwell.
   Like pebbles pile-heaped they dwell, ever dwell.

Among the researchers of Australian aboriginal culture, it is generally agreed that aboriginal music may be classified as secret, sacred or secular.

The secret chants are always performed in a secret place (a shrine, a temple or other hallowed ground) and relate to the tribe's mythology, dogma and ancestor-heroes. The initiated men are the only persons attending and performing at these ceremonies. It is the Headman of the cult who is in authority here.

The sacred (really semi-sacred) songs may be heard on the campground, on special occasions, with both men and women participating. Again it is the Headman who assumes the role of leader here, unless he delegates his authority to another.

The only aboriginal music that can be performed at any time, at any place, and by any person are the secular songs and dances. This folklore may concern itself with recent or past occurrences, articles used every day, love songs, nature and its phenomena, or gossip, more by insinuation than by direct reference.

These songs for pure entertainment are traded freely from tribe to tribe. If perchance they cross language borders, the new recipients may not understand the meaning of the words, but that matters little; perhaps the dance and mime employed will suggest the idea.

The most publicized of these aboriginal social occasions is the corroboree. It is here that the Songman shows that he is a unifying and integrating factor in his clan. Night after night, these folk song and dance "happenings" bring together the entire group—young and old, male and female. Let us attend one of these corroborees along with A. P. Elkin, as he picturesquely describes such an evening.

"During the day, members of the group have been scattered on their economic and other activities, either in their own indigenous way or in relation to white men. Evening comes and a meal is eaten in family groups. Then as darkness descends and camp fires sparkle, a didjeridoo and the tapping of sticks are heard from the dance-place or the Songman's camp. Gradually and casually men and women move over to the cleared ground. Perhaps someone, hearing the preliminary sounds, has eagerly called out 'corroboree over there'—a Wongga, a Walaka, a Gunborg or other dance title. Arriving there ourselves, we see the Songman sitting or standing (according to the song and dance), with his rhythm sticks in his hands, singing and beating time. Alongside of him is a didjeridoo player or 'puller' as he is called, producing a deep note of varied rhythm from a hollowed piece of wood about six feet long and two or three feet internal diameter. He takes his cue from the Songman. The latter may be assisted by one or more singers, but he is the leader—determining what is to be sung, and if there be an unaccompanied recitative at the end, he is the last to finish.

Further, we see some young men and some not so young, and a few boys, dancing in ballet style. They enter the dance place from the side of the ground opposite to the Songman, and dance toward him, raising dust with their accented stamping. There may be a leading dancer, but he and his fellows are under the general direction of the Songman, who is Master of ceremonies. On one edge of the ground, too, just after each song and dance commence, some women and girls stand up and, without shifting their position, rhythmically move their feet, legs and arms in time with the music. They are just as intent on their silent dancing as are the more active men, and may be praised as good dancers. Nearby in the various camps, old folk and parents with little ones on their knees listen and watch, and beat the rhythm.

Thus all are brought together as one in the rhythm of the song, didjeridoo and dance—a rhythm which is timeless, linking generation to generation as dancers in one great corroboree."

(Top) Aboriginal Corroboree ground at Yuendumu, Northern Territory, in central Australia. *(Bottom)* At Yirrkalla, on the Arnhem Land Aboriginal Reservation in the Northern Territory, aboriginal men gather to chant songs of aboriginal beliefs. Music is provided by the didjeridoo, a hollow stick eaten out by termites.

(Courtesy of Australian News and Information Bureau)

(Top) A group of nomadic aborigines, in ceremonial paint, performing one of their ancient ritual dances, known as Corroborees. *(Bottom)* A Corroboree, photographed by the Barclay Expedition to the Northern Territory in 1911.

(Courtesy of Australian News and Information Bureau)

Young aboriginal dancers rehearse in Darwin for the 1970 North Australian Eisteddford. An aboriginal dancing section has been included in the Eisteddford at Darwin since 1963.

(Courtesy of Australian News and Information Bureau)

FOR FURTHER READING

The Australian News and Information Bureau, 636 Fifth Ave., New York, N. Y. 10020 (or Box 12, Post Office, Canberra, Australia) have available interesting booklets and other literature, including:

Australian Panorama—colorful with pictures.

Australia in Brief—concise and full of up-to-date, useful information.

The latest research relating to the aborigines may be obtained upon request from the Australian Institute of Aboriginal Studies, Box 553, Canberra A.C.T., Australia.

A limited listing of books on the history and music of Australia, and the English language as it is spoken "Down Under," follows:

Baker, S.J.: *The Australian Language,* Currawong, Sydney and Tri-Ocean Books, San Francisco, 1966.

Barnard, M.F.: *A History of Australia,* Praeger, New York, 1963.

Berndt & Ronald & Murray: *Aboriginal Man in Australia,* Angus and Robertson, Cremorne Jct. N.S.W., Australia, 1965.

Brander, B. & Harrell, M.A. & Holthouse, H.: *Australia,* Special Publications Division, National Geographic Society, Washington, D.C., 1968.

Clark, C.M.H.: *A History of Australia,* Melbourne University Press, Melbourne, 1962.

Clark, C.M.H.: *A Short History of Australia,* New American Library, New York, 1963.

Covell, R.: *Australia's Music-Themes of a New Society,* Sun Books, Melbourne, 1967.

Elkin, A.P. & Jones, T.A.: *Arnhem Land Music,* University of Sydney, Sydney, 1958.

Elkin, A.P.: *The Australian Aborigines* (in cooperation with the Museum of Natural History) Doubleday, New York, 1964.

Greenwood, G.: *Australia—A Social and Political History*, Angus and Robertson, Cremorne Jct. N.S.W., Australia, 1955.

MacInnes, C. & Editors of Life-Time, Inc.: *Australia and New Zealand*, Time Inc., New York, 1961.

Manifold, J.S.: *Penguin Australian Song Book*, Penguin Books, Ringwood, Victoria, Australia, 1964.

McLeod, A.L., Editor: *The Pattern of Australian Culture*, Cornell University Press, Ithaca, New York, 1963.

Mendelsohn, O.A.: *A Waltz With Matilda*, Lansdowne Press, Melbourne, 1966.

Pike, D.H.: *Australia—The Quiet Continent*, Cambridge University Press, London, 1962.

Reese, T.R.: *Australia in the Twentieth Century*, Praeger, New York, 1964.

Shaw, A.G.L.: *A Short History of Australia*, Praeger, New York, 1967.

Strehlow, T.G.H.: *Aboriginal Songs of Central Australia*, Angus and Robertson, Cremorne Jct. N.S.W., Australia, 1971.

Tennant, E.: *Australia—Her Story*, Macmillan, London, 1953.

Tindale, N. and Lindsay, H.A.: *Aboriginal Australia*, Angus and Robertson, Cremorne Jct. N.S.W., Australia, 1963.

Turnbull, C.M.: *A Concise History of Australia*, Viking Press, New York, 1965.

Tyson, R.: *The Australian Christmas Book*, Lansdowne Press, Melbourne, 1965.

The Bibliography of any scholarly book will include additional listings, which will extend the scope of this volume.

FOR LISTENING

Folkways Records— 701 Seventh Ave., New York, N.Y. 10036
  4102 *Songs of Aboriginal Australia and Torres Strait*
  4210 *Songs of the Western Australian Desert Aborigines*
  4439 *Tribal Music of Australia*
  8718 *Australian Folksongs and Ballads*

Monitor Records— 156 Fifth Ave., New York, N.Y. 10010
  424 *Waltzing Matilda*

Available in Australia
  Australian Record Co. Ltd. — 11 Hargrave St., East Sydney, N.S.W. 2010
    This Australia—Australian Bush Songs and Poetry, including two Aboriginal Chants

Alice M. Moyle has compiled an invaluable and comprehensive *Handlist of Field Collections of Recorded Music in Australia and the Torres Strait* for the Australian Institute of Aboriginal Studies, Canberra, P.O.B. 553 A.C.T. 2601, Australia—1966.

Koala Bears.

*(Courtesy of "Australian Panorama" - an Australian
News and Information Bureau Publication)*

A LIST OF AUSTRALIAN WORDS
AS USED IN THIS BOOK

Backblock: Originally, a block of land in a remote section of a cattle station. As these became populated, it referred to any inland area.

Back-of-the-beyond: The most remote and rugged or barren regions of Australia.

Bandicoot: A marsupial (having a pouch for carrying the young), about the size of a rabbit, which like them, may have large ears and long hind legs.

Bellbird: A thrushlike bird of two distinct types. The Bellminer develops its song as a group. One bird sings "dink," another follows, and so a bell-like song is developed. The Crested Bellbird is a solo performer noted for its airy, melodious song.

Billy: . . .is of aboriginal origin—"billa," a creek or river. Transferring this meaning to "water," a billy is a tin in which water is boiled, and also used for boiling vegetables and for stewing.

Billabong: . . .of aboriginal origin—"billa," a creek or river, "bong," dead. Hence, a river or creek no longer running—a water hole.

Blued: One of those terms in the Australian language that has gathered to itself many meanings. In the context used in these songs, it means to spend foolishly and extravagantly.

Brolga: A grey plumaged, slimly built crane, noted for its high flights and its group dances. The word is of aboriginal origin.

Bullocky: The driver of a bullock team.

Bush: The country beyond the populated areas.

Bushrangers: Bush bandits.

Coolibah tree: The eucalyptus tree.

Currawong: A black and white "scrub-magpie" is not, along with the sparrow and starling, protected by law. These outlawed birds, it seems, are still flourishing.

Dingo: A gray or yellow dog of European or Asiatic wolf-type, coming to Australia centuries ago with the aborigines. Living in the hills and plains, it preys on marsupials, and more recently on rabbits and sometimes on lambs.

Dronga: A black and white, insect eating, aggressive bird. The word is of aboriginal origin.

Duffer: A cattle thief.

Free Selector: A would-be farmer.

Friar bird: An aggressive, black and white species; one of the chattering, gabbling "peculiar voices" of Australian birds.

Gammoned: Tricked into a deal by falsehood.

Goana: . . .of aboriginal origin—a lizard, about six feet in length.

Grazier: A squatter—a sheep raiser.

Gum tree: The eucalyptus tree.

Gun: An expert shearer—one who shears over two hundred sheep a day.

Hump his drum: The Derwenters were shearers who were distinguished by their tall hats and kangaroo knapsacks or Derwent "drums."

Hump his swag:	To carry his knapsack or "swag" (supplies rolled in a blanket) on his back.
Jumbuck:	A sheep.
Koala Bear:	Together with the kangaroo, a "trade mark" of Australia. The gray-furred marsupial (having a pouch for carrying its young) frequents trees, feeding on the leaves of the eucalyptus tree.
Kookaburra:	A bird belonging to the kingfisher family. It is sometimes called "Laughing Jackass" because of its call sounding like raucous laughter.
Lorikeet:	. . .also known as the Honey-Parrot, designating to which family it belongs. There are eight native species of parrots today, ranging in color from blue, red and yellow to green. They go squawking from area to area as seasons change, feeding on blossoms of the gum tree and, at times, attacking fruit in orchards.
Matilda:	A bundle (swag) on a stick carried by a swagman.
Neddies:	Race horses.
New Australian:	Post World War II migrants, including Italians, Germans, Greeks, Dutch, from practically every free European country, with a preponderance of those of British stock.
Outback:	Vast and rugged regions of the country.
Pint pot:	One half of a "quart pot," a synonym for a billy.
Pannekin:	A small pan or cup.
Ringer:	The champion shearer in a shearing shed.
Ryebuck:	An especially good shearer.
Selection:	Land selected by a would-be-farmer (a free selector).

Sheila: A girl; a dame.

Snagger: An inferior shearer, one who is learning the trade or perhaps an older worker.

Squatter: In early colonial days, one who illegally took possession of land. Later, in the middle or late nineteenth century, a sheep raiser or grazier.

Station: A cattle ranch.

Stock whip: The whip used by a stockman, usually made of kangaroo hide with the thongs eight to ten feet long, with the cord or "cracker" made of horse hair.

Swag: See "hump his swag."

Swagman: The nomad who "humps his swag."

Tally: As either noun or verb, it is used in relation to the counting of sheep.

Tucker: Food or meal.

Woodlark: One of a large family noted for its song.

Zarucker: Trooper.

READERS' NOTES